A Case for Creation

A Case for Creation

by

Wayne Frair
and
Percival Davis

Illustrated by Carla Field

Library of Congress Cataloging in Publication Data
Frair, Wayne.
  A case for creation.
  Includes bibliographical references and index.
  1. Creationism. 2. Evolution. I. Davis, P. William.
II. Title.
BS651.F74 1983   231.7'65   82-23998
ISBN 0-8024-0176-7

3 4 5 6 7 Printing/BB/Year 88 87 86

Printed in the United States of America

CONTENTS

FOREWORD

A Case for Creation appears at a time when the controversy between those who support creation and those who believe in evolution is becoming increasingly bitter and emotional. Emotions are heating up as individuals and the general public are asked to choose sides on the matter of what approach should be taken in our public schools.

Part of this emotionalism is the result of misrepresentations of the creationist position, but more significant is that creationism represents an attack on the belief system of many in the scientific community. In some quarters evolution has become the party line to be defended at all costs. Also contributing to the emotionalism of the argument is science's image of being absolutely objective. If indeed it is a logical, rational system, then there should be no disagreement on conclusions. The attacks that have been raised by Paul Feyerabend on modern science and the scientific method are therefore disconcerting. He believes that modern science now occupies a position in Western society incommensurate with the free exchange of ideas and the further development of science, and he argues that equal weight should be given to competing avenues of knowledge. His criticisms need to be heard even though we may not agree with his suggestions of alternate avenues of knowledge.

Much more important for the controversy between creation and evolution, however, is the disconcerting fact that the genius of modern science, controlled experimentation, cannot be applied to a study of the past. It is simply impossible to reproduce the conditions of the past to determine if they could indeed bring about the changes assigned to them. Moreover, we are handicapped by the impossibility of compressing a great deal of time into our laboratory studies. Because of these inherent defects the theory of evolution can never have the validity and reliability of scientific conclusions about current phenomena; many of its explanations can be little more than interesting conjectures.

There are cogent arguments in support of the idea of a sudden origin in time of a wide variety of living things. There is also evidence that a limited amount of change has taken place in the living world. The authors of *A Case for Creation* have attempted to marshal evidence for that conclusion in certain areas of biology. They also suggest that exploration of other areas may result in more evidence to support the conclusion of limited change.

The authors also plead for additional research by creationists. They point out that in the past we have often been content to take a negative approach. Little research has been done by creationists, to some extent because they have been excluded by anticreationist bias from participation in the scientific enterprise. Frair and Davis believe that the time has come for a substantial amount of research by those who support the idea of a sudden origin of a variety of living things. It is not enough merely to point out the flaws in the theory of evolution; research is needed that will support the ideas and explanations espoused by creationists.

We hope this plea will not go unheard.

John W. Klotz, Ph.D.
Director, School for Graduate Studies
Concordia Theological Seminary
St. Louis, Missouri

PREFACE

Numerous books on evolution have been written in recent years, including some works treating evolutionary theory from a more-or-less Christian point of view. Since one might well question the need for yet another addition to the already-voluminous literature of scientific apologetics, we believe that a word of explanation is in order.

Recent attempts to include creationism in public school teachings of origins have created a sense of misplaced confidence. If we are to battle for men's souls, we must not neglect their minds. It is futile to expose students or anyone else to unconvincing concepts. In our opinion, creationists must carefully set forth a case for creation with all the care and skill that a lawyer would use to convince a skeptical jury. Perhaps this little book may help those concerned with this issue to formulate their ideas logically and to present them effectively and constructively.

It is an illusion to suppose that the problems evolutionary doctrine raises for the Christian are well under control. Such a supposition could be a very dangerous misconception. The Christian who is at ease regarding evolution is one who has no understanding of the true scope of the evangelical dilemma in this field of study. The doctrine of evolution in its present form is the creation of men of genius. To underestimate it and its impact is dangerous.

It is our aim to enter a plea for increased research by Christians concerning the origins of life on Earth and Earth's subsequent history. We also want to urge a creative reinterpretation that is biblically harmonious with what is already known. If this book stimulates either the initiation of well-conceived research programs or scholarly studies, it will have amply repaid our efforts.

We are not sympathetic, however, with the approach that

attempts to apply Scripture haphazardly to the latest fashions of intellect or science. It is our firm conviction that Scripture must be allowed to speak to man and that man must not presume to dictate to Scripture. We are not attempting to interpret (or misinterpret) the Bible so that it speaks the language of the twentieth-century geologist or zoologist. That approach might impress naive Christians, but it would not be accepted outside the church. In the long run it would defeat its own purpose by leaving the enemy in uncontested possession of the battlefield. Such an attempt really constitutes a search for the most graceful means of surrender.

It has been no part of our plan, incidentally, to redefine the vocabulary of science in accordance with our own preconceptions. Recent years have seen entirely too much of that sort of semantic juggling, and we believe it is in large measure responsible for the rampant intellectual confusion seen everywhere (among Christians also). Thus, when we use the terms *evolution, hypothesis, history,* and *creation,* we intend to mean just what the consensus of past and present users of those terms have meant. And we have not attempted to coin neologisms that are supposedly superior to those terms in general use. One tower of Babel was enough.

Finally, we have designed this book principally for the informed layman and the student in his early years of scientific training. Accordingly, we decided to use a minimum of footnotes throughout. This has limited the scholarly scope of our treatment, but it is hoped the book's readability will be increased. Those who would delve more deeply into the subject should consult standard works, such as those listed in the selected bibliography.

We have omitted certain topics and treated others with great brevity (e.g., space science and strictly geological matters, such as dating and the Genesis Flood). We are biologists and we believe that extensive discussion of those specialized topics should be the responsibility of experts. We have dealt with them only when they are essential to an understanding of the biological topics under consideration. (The anecdotes on pp. 30-31 and 133-34 were supplied by Percival Davis.)

We gratefully acknowledge the assistance of Mrs. Karen Y. Davis for her innumerable stylistic and grammatical corrections, as well as more substantive editorial help and manuscript preparation. Suggestions, encouragement, and aid in improving this edition have come from many, including Ronald J. Burwell, Russell R. Camp, Ruth Prol, Ruth Redel, and Howard Vos.

1

EVOLUTION AND SCIENCE

Every age has possessed certain unquestioned presuppositions that served as foundations for its most popular philosophies. Such a presupposition in our day is the theory of evolution. This concept has become the basis of much scientific and political theory, formal philosophy, and even theology. Evolutionary thought appears to be a cornerstone of modern civilization. If this is the case, surely we ought to examine such a cornerstone with care. If it is defective, the consequences one day could be disastrous. Disturbing evidence is accumulating that it has been unwise for us to allow this doctrine of evolution to become so foundational—it may be partially or wholly untrue.

In many high schools and colleges today evolution is nevertheless treated as fact. The evolutionary theory is indeed the product of men of genius and is the result of more than a century of intense and serious intellectual effort. Its very bulk and elaborateness is intellectually intimidating. To the beginning student it seems an impregnable structure, for he is without the knowledge and experience to criticize it. This book is written to show that evolutionary doctrine is wrong. An alternative position is presented in order to challenge concerned individuals to discover more adequate explanations for the origins of living things.

The prevalent feeling in Western culture in recent centuries has been that the general growth and positive progress of things was inevitable. To be sure, we do see all kinds of human activities and organizations starting from small and humble origins and increasing in complexity. We have the feeling, perhaps unconsciously, that there is development and evolution in our world, for one meaning of the word *evolution* is "systematic development from the simple to the complex." *Biological evolution*, therefore, usually refers to a progression in organisms from simple to relatively complex.

Living organisms and extinct fossil forms are thought to be descendants of a relatively simple, self-reproducing chemical or protoplasmic substance.

DARWINISM

When Charles Darwin more than a century ago published his book *The Origin of Species,* people were in the mood to hail it as what seemed to be the first totally acceptable explanation for the origin and development of living things. However, Darwin's theory of biological evolution was not completely original. There are rather ambiguous traces of the beginnings of evolutionary thought in writings of Greeks such as Thales, Anaximander, Empedocles, and Aristotle, hundreds of years before Christ. Nevertheless, it was not until the revival of classical and scientific learning in the seventeenth and eighteenth centuries that new ideas were added to the ancient concepts. This paved the way for the acceptance of Darwinism, supported as it was by a vast array of original observations that had been largely lacking in previous works.

The Origin of Species went through five revisions at Darwin's hand. Darwin presented in it and in other writings his conclusions regarding the development of life. In reading Darwin, one receives a distinct impression that he was almost compulsive in his endeavor to keep abreast of the latest discoveries and generally to face scientific issues fairly. His writings contain good scientific data, much of which is still acceptable today. However, some of his writings have been shown to be incorrect or at least open to considerable question in the light of modern knowledge. Products of their era, his works lack information on cytology (study of cells), physiology (study of function), and, of course, the newer sciences of biochemistry, biophysics, and biomathematics. For this reason the works cannot be accepted as valid in all modern scientific aspects.

Some of Darwin's embryological beliefs are now known to be untrue. Many of his anthropological ideas, such as those regarding the development of religion and language, have been shown to be incorrect. His ideas on the relationship between intelligence and sex are rejected today by competent psychologists. (Although some males still cling to them tenaciously!) He stated, for example, that "the average of mental power in man must be above that of woman," and that through sexual selection "man has ultimately become superior to woman."[1]

---

1. Charles Darwin, *The Origin of Species and the Descent of Man* (New York: Random House, 1971), 2:873-74.

Many of those strange ideas were related to his erroneous concepts regarding heredity. He invented bodies known as *gemmules* in order to account (as he thought) for observed hereditary data. Understandably, modern concepts of heredity involving genetic ratios, chromosome studies, deoxyribonucleic acid (DNA), and many other new concepts are very different from anything Darwin could have proposed.

Darwin's evolutionary ideas were accepted by many scientists of his day, but a considerable number of great scientists, including Owen, von Baer, Wigand, Agassiz, and Sedgwick, rejected his theories. Today no informed scientist believes exactly as Darwin did, but the most popular current evolutionary views are still Darwinian in essence. It is undeniable that the major features of Darwin's evolutionary thought have endured.

Although the doctrine of evolution was presented to account for changes among living things, its implications have been extended into the sociological, political, and religious realms. For example, Darwin's teachings have been extended to justify taking unfair advantage of others. Known as Social Darwinism, this idea was expounded by Herbert Spencer even before Darwin published his ideas. Spencer imagined an evolutionary struggle at all levels, in which the greatest advancement was secured by ruthless and unethical competition. In this way, by analogy with animal competition and "survival of the fittest," many unscrupulous activities were justified. Teachings of such leaders as Nietzsche and Hitler have contained ideas consistent with Social Darwinism and apparently derived from it. Fortunately, this viewpoint is not currently popular in the Western world.

Another popular belief that grew out of Darwin's writings held "wild" tribes to be composed of people who were intermediate between apes and civilized man. Many people thought culture (including religion) had evolved through a series of patterns that were all evident among living peoples. According to this teaching, lineal cultural evolution began with the savages. But recent studies in cultural anthropology have indicated that regardless of the degree of civilization, members of the human race possess a basic physiological, psychological, and spiritual unity.

For instance, whereas the popular nineteenth-century view held so-called primitive or Stone Age men to be intermediate between apes and modern Europeans with regard to language, arts, and intelligence, it is now recognized that their languages are often more intricate and expressive than our own. Great skill is evidenced in much of their drawing, carving, weaving, and pottery.

Their music is often of complex and subtle rhythmic structure, though we may not appreciate it because our ears are attuned to our own concepts of melody and harmony. The culture of Stone Age men living 7,000 years ago was at least as sophisticated as that of many "primitive" tribes of today. In these tribes, as in all cultures of living men, there is belief in the supernatural and in life after death. When adequate testing procedures are used, the intelligence of "primitive" peoples approximates our own. This presence of intelligence and human culture practically and readily distinguishes man from all animals.

Do modern scientific advances depend on the theory of evolution and require an acceptance of its tenets? There seems to be no good reason to insist that biological studies always be informed by evolutionary considerations. What recent important biological achievement could not have been accomplished just as well without a belief in evolution on the investigator's part?

During the twentieth century many of the erroneous early presuppositions of evolutionary anthropology have been corrected. So the chief scientific quest in anthropology today is certainly not the determination of which human race is most like the apes, but rather the main area of study is the current diversified patterns of human culture and physique. The most fruitful scientific endeavors in anthropology have been those conducted *within* the family of man.

Similarly, in recent years there has been a growing tendency in many areas (e.g., taxonomy) to use other than evolutionary approaches to scientific data. This has happened because of the misapplication of Darwinism as it spread, and because many exceptions to evolutionary generalizations have been found.

Such scientific studies of current, specific groups of animals are, for the most part, scientifically valid because the results may be verified much more objectively than those studies that have attempted to relate diverse kinds of organisms.

On the other hand, general similarities that exist among members of different groups such as dogs and rabbits, or cats and mice are certainly important. We acknowledge this every time experimental drugs are tested on laboratory rats, mice, or monkeys. Why not perform such tests on lizards or spiders? Because it is obvious that animals most similar to us in a variety of ways can be expected to be most similar to us also in their response to medication. Such similarities can be explained as originating in basic design given by the Creator. Evolution is not necessary to account for the similarities.

The Nature of Science

There are many reasons for Darwinism's widespread misapplication and its present unfortunate position of prominence in the scientific world. One of the important reasons for this situation is that the methods and techniques of science are not well understood—in many cases, not even by practicing scientists themselves. Until recently the prestige of science has been nearly absolute, and often a statement that something is "scientific" has been taken by the layman to mean it is *certain*. Scientific "facts" of the last twenty years, for instance, held that burns were to be treated with butter or salve (never water) and that Jupiter was a cold planet. These and countless other widely held "facts" are believed by no one today.

Science itself differs from the products of science. Most of the technological differences between today and the past are because of improved scientific methods for exploiting the environment. The products of science are, from a practical point of view, *tools*. The use of most of these tools, such as bulldozers or airplanes, is obvious. A theory also can be considered a useful tool, a key to nature that opens up new roads to knowledge. However, because it *is* a tool, any theory has certain limitations. It must be used intelligently, it should be improved as knowledge accumulates, and it should fall into disuse when a more effective tool is invented. Let us consider the origin of theories and their use, for these are the most basic tools of science.

THE SCIENTIFIC METHOD

What is it that makes science "scientific"? Dictionary definitions center on the idea of systematic classification and careful collection of data, which is usually assembled into coherent wholes. All these are important aspects of science, but by no means give the essentials of science. Most scientists would insist that an acceptable definition would have to include the concept of the *scientific method*. But such a definition is circular. What is the scientific method?

The scientific method is a hybrid of two main forms of thought— *deduction* and *induction*. Deduction is probably the most common form of inferential logic in which the necessary consequences of a fact are determined. Induction is the means by which we interpret observations and assess their significance. It is the process of forming generalizations. The drawback of induction is that it can be used too subjectively. It is easy to make erroneous generalizations, especially when they are drawn from insufficient data. Yet who is to say that he is in possession of all relevant data? Since the answer is obviously "No one," it follows that induction is inherently fallible.

Yet induction is a cornerstone of the scientific method. We *must* employ induction, for deduction is parasitic upon it. The only way we obtain the raw material of reason is to make observations and generalize upon them. The scholastic philosophers of the high Middle Ages appreciated this dilemma and proposed a partial solution. Why not combine the two, they reasoned. One could propose a tentative generalization called a *hypothesis.* The logical consequences of that hypothesis could then be inferred deductively, and those consequences could be tested against reality by further observation. If the consequences were true, the hypothesis could be tentatively accepted; if false, the hypothesis could be rejected.

This method has survived and has become the basis for all modern science. All science must involve the proposal of a testable hypothesis, the inference of its consequences, and the attempt to match those consequences with the real universe by observation. Thus a hypothesis is a proposed explanation for some problem or phenomenon that catches the attention of the scientist, and a prediction is one of the logical consequences of that hypothesis. Predictions are confirmed, or not, by attempted observation. To generate the necessary observations, scientists usually design controlled experiments.

Perhaps the characteristics of a genuine hypothesis that most distinguish it from dogma on the one hand and speculation on the other are that a hypothesis is *tentative* and *falsifiable.* That is, a hypothesis must be explicitly understood to be uncertain when it is proposed, and it should suggest predictions that will be observed not only if it is true, *but also if it is false.*

One of the chief difficulties of the scientific method is that false hypotheses often appear true because by coincidence they sometimes suggest true predictions. In the early days of the germ theory of disease, for instance, it was suggested that the microbes found in infected wounds did not cause the infection but were permitted to develop there as a consequence of the inflammation. The hypothesis that the microbes are a consequence of the disease did suggest the prediction that they would usually be found in disease states, and so it is. Despite this true prediction, the hypothesis was shown to be false when experimental injuries were inflicted under sterile conditions. When that was done, the microbes and inflammation both failed to appear. That is exactly what one would predict if the hypothesis was false.

One cannot know whether a hypothesis is false except by inferring its logical consequences in the foregoing way. If they are demonstrably false, then the hypothesis is necessarily false. But oddly enough, as we have seen, the reverse cannot be said. A false hypothesis can suggest true predictions by coincidence, but a true hypothesis cannot suggest false predictions. That means that the falsification of a hypothesis can be trusted, but not its verification. This leads us to the conclusion that the scientific method is basically negative. It can be used to attempt to prune away some of the untruths we propose, but it cannot assure us of the validity of the remainder.

What makes the scientific method work despite this is that if a false hypothesis should suggest a true conclusion, it *must* be by coincidence. By definition, a *coincidence* is an unlikely chance occurrence. Such an occurrence is even less likely to occur twice or several times. Thus, if we observe a prediction that is consistent with a hypothesis, we should consider that as encouraging, but not as indicating the hypothesis is true. We must try to make other kinds of predictions and test them in their turn. If several such predictions come to pass as expected, the hypothesis is probably (but not certainly) true. Note, however, that because the essence of a scientific hypothesis is its falsifiability, a hypothesis that is proposed in such a way that it *cannot* possibly or practically be discredited, *even if it is untrue,* lies outside the scope of the scientific method. It could be true in fact, but it is scientifically undemonstrable; and it is thus not really a hypothesis at all. Such proposals are usually called *unfalsifiable hypotheses.*

PREDICTION AND RETRODICTION

Must predictions be observed in future time? The ordinary meaning of the word would suggest it, but there is a variety of "prediction" that is a consequential event observable as a *past* occurrence. We shall call such a reverse prediction a *retrodiction.*

Past events have had consequences in time that was future time for the events, but past or present for us. The American Revolution led to the War of 1812, which otherwise would not have taken place as it did. If someone were to doubt that the American Revolution took place, but could be convinced that the War of 1812 did take place, he could perhaps be convinced on that basis that the American Revolution was a historic fact. In principle, then, it should be possible to erect testable hypotheses about events that may have occurred in the past. Then one could deduce the consequences and search for evidence that they had occurred.

Of the two methods, prediction has much greater falsifying power than retrodiction for two reasons: (1) it is always possible to claim that failure to find evidence of a retrodiction has resulted from chance loss, and (2) it is possible to claim that an unavailable class of evidence is needed to discredit the hypothesis. The upshot is that historic hypotheses are likely to become unfalsifiable hypotheses. Put differently, it is often possible to choose predictions to test the most crucial aspects of a hypothesis, but with retrodictions one is stuck with events that have already occurred, and among those, only the ones whose remains can be detected today. Needless to say, the past has not been designed as a logical instrument for our use. It is certainly not open to experimentation.

DIFFICULTIES WITH RETRODICTION

Let us consider an example. One of the great chestnuts of paleontology has been what caused the dinosaurs to become extinct. The really odd aspects of the situation are supposed to be the suddenness with which extinction took place, its thoroughness, and other widespread, simultaneous extinctions, such as that of the trilobites. According to conventional paleontology, the dinosaurs lasted for about 100 million years; according to more recent and less conventional paleontology, they may have become extinct in a period as short as ten years, or even less. If that were true, it would be difficult to name a catastrophe that could have eliminated them so quickly and so thoroughly.

Numerous ones have nevertheless been suggested, some quite sensational: (1) a nearby supernova, for instance, could have saturated the earth with lethal radiation; (2) the Arctic Ocean, if initially landlocked, could have been released by geological events, spreading over the more saline water of the warmer seas and producing drastic climatic changes, including a ten-year, near-absolute drought; (3) an asteroid or comet might have collided with the earth, producing (in addition to tidal waves and earthquakes) atmospheric dust that would have obscured the sun. By interfering with photosynthesis, this would have killed all but a few plants, although presumably seeds would have survived. With the resultant collapse of all terrestrial and aquatic food chains upon which dinosaurs and other organisms were dependent, the dinosaurs would have become extinct.

Noncatastrophic explanations have also been advanced, such as flowering plants displacing the gymnosperms that dinosaurs were specially adapted to eat. One version of that theory holds that the gymnosperms contained a cathartic substance without which the dinosaurs died of massive constipation! Each of this plethora of proposals has its advocates and detractors. How can one hope to distinguish among them?

A June 6, 1980 article in *Science* magazine, "Extraterrestrial Cause for the Cretaceous-Tertiary Extinction," by Luis Alvarez, Walter Alvarez, Frank Asaro, and Helen V. Michel proposed that a key to the extinction problem is that rocks formed at the time have abnormally high concentrations of platinum-like metals, especially iridium. This metal, rare in earthly surface rocks, is much more richly concentrated in meteorites and presumably in asteroids also. This fact suggested to Alvarez and his colleagues that the high concentrations of iridium in the late Cretaceous rocks may have resulted from the collision of the earth with an asteroid. This collision also would have resulted in the extinctions because of reduced photosynthesis, as already mentioned. Could the iridium have another explanation? Could it have come from the exploding supernova, as rival theorists might suggest? No, for if that were the case, calculations should show that the iridium is accompanied by comparable quantities of a plutonium isotope, and such is not the case.

Alvarez and his colleagues seemed to have made a good case for their asteroidal bomb, until a series of letters appeared in subsequent issues of *Science* (as February 13, 1981). In one of those, Dennis V. Kent pointed out that iridium concentrations such as Alvarez et al. found so remarkable are not all that uncommon in rocks of varying ages and locales. Recall that Alvarez et al. believed an asteroid collision released dust that interfered with photosynthesis. Many sedimentary rocks are dependent on living organisms for their formation and hence are directly or indirectly dependent on photosynthesis. Kent reversed this causality and suggested that reduced sediment deposition, resulting perhaps from something else entirely, would have the effect of concentrating iridium in a smaller total volume of rock, in these thinner layers, thus increasing its concentration. As a final blow, Kent referred to "fossil" volcanic eruptions, some of whose craters are known to approach a size of 35 kilometers by 100 kilometers, completely dwarfing that of Krakatoa, to say nothing of Mt. St. Helens. One of those, the Toba caldera in Sumatra, probably ejected some 2,000 cubic kilometers of material into the atmosphere, an amount more than sufficient to suppress earthly photosynthesis. That eruption is supposed to have occurred about 25,000 years B.P. (before present times), a time that paleontologists have not named as a time of massive extinctions.

To these points another correspondent, George C. Reid, added that "Under these extreme conditions [such as those posited by Alvarez] the problem becomes not one of explaining the extinction of half the genera living at the time, but one of explaining the survival of the other half."

Consider how Alvarez's hypothesis was proposed and tested in this typical example of retrodiction, and consider the results, if any. The problem was to account for the apparent massive extinction of late Cretaceous life, which extinction had never been satisfactorily explained. The hypothesis was that dust injected into the atmosphere by an asteroidal collision produced the extinctions by interfering with photosynthesis, thus cutting off all food chains at the source. This hypothesis suggested a family of retrodictions and Alvarez produced one: iridium would be deposited in a particular concentration in the sediments of that time. That retrodiction is indeed true, at least apparently, and Alvarez takes that truth as confirmation of his hypothesis.

Kent, however, infers two other less happy retrodictions. First, he points out that if high iridium concentrations are to be taken as evidence of asteroidal collision, they should occur only in conjunction with catastrophes. But that does not seem to be the case, because such concentrations are widely distributed throughout the geological record. So there is no reason to associate the Cretaceous case examined by Alvarez with an asteroidal collision. It could easily have been produced by a coincidental occurrence of some kind. Second, Kent says if Alvarez's hypothetical asteroid killed the dinosaurs by turning off the light, so should massive volcanic eruptions. But there is no evidence that light ever was cut off, despite clear indications that such eruptions have occurred in the past. Reid adds another contradictory retrodiction: such a horrific event should have nearly wiped out late Cretaceous life, but that does not seem to have occurred either.

Have we then been able to rule out conclusively the asteroid collision hypothesis? Not at all. Quite undiscouraged, Alvarez replied to these criticisms in a familiar vein—further research is needed. Perhaps it is, but for the moment it appears that this attempted application of the scientific method to past events has produced a classic unfalsifiable hypothesis that, although *perhaps* it could be true, cannot be dealt with by means of the scientific method. The final word may have been spoken by yet another correspondent, whose letter to *Science* suggested that the issue had already been examined in a more enjoyable way—in the aptly-named Walt Disney film *Fantasia*.

Despite all this, the asteroid collision hypothesis seems well on its way to becoming an accepted scientific dogma. Articles in periodicals ranging from *The New York State Conservationist* to *Scientific American* have burst into print, most without a hint of the afore-mentioned objections. It has even made prime-time television.

So it is hard to know what data could be used (or whether any still survive) that would enable us to decide which, if any, of the hypotheses is correct. In fact, it could have been caused by a flood! But one would be rash indeed who would suggest that a flood could be demonstrated by retrodiction.

From the foregoing discussion it should be clear that the scientific method is a practical device for resolving questions in "real time." It is far less effective when applied to the past, and for that reason it is doubtful that the general concept of biological evolution is falsifiable by the scientific method. Certain aspects of the theory *can* be studied in real time in the laboratory or field, but as we shall see, those studies have not demonstrated that evolution is true in the general sense, that is, that it has produced the world of life as we know it today. To the extent that it can be demonstrated to be true at all, evolution can be shown to be only trivially true.

Is Creationism Scientific?

What of creationism? Is it "scientific," or can it be made so? Strictly speaking, the answer is no. Despite the insistence by proponents that evolution is firmly established as scientific, its dependence on retrodiction greatly weakens that claim. By criticizing evolution as unscientific, however, one does not thereby establish creationism as scientific—*and this should not bother us!* Science is a practical tool for approximating truth. Though there is probably no influence more pervasive in our society than science, and though it has produced a revolution in human thought unprecedented in history, science is not infallible. Truth, in fact, takes precedence over science. Let creationists frankly acknowledge that their commitment to creation depends at least as much on faith[2] as on science. The evolutionists are no better off. We can and should exceed them in honesty.

Theory and Truth

When sufficient information on a topic accumulates, the scientist attempts to make a *generalization*. A generalization is a statement

---

2. As Hebrews 11:3 puts it, "*By faith* [not scientific data] we understand that the worlds were prepared by the word of God" (italics added).

encompassing all observed data in summary form. The earliest form of a generalization is termed a *hypothesis*. When observations confirming a hypothesis accumulate, the hypothesis becomes a *theory*. A theory unchallenged and consistently supported by facts is called a *law* after a considerable lapse of time.

This process of moving from generalization to law does not necessarily mean the generalization has become fact; the likelihood of its being correct merely increases, or, as it is commonly stated, it has a higher statistical probability of being right. If any observation (even though seemingly trivial) conflicts with the generalization or hypothesis, the scientist is left with two major alternatives: (1) discard the hypothesis and search for another, or (2) attempt to find some plausible explanation for the observation in accord with the hypothesis. There is no major scientific hypothesis of any age that has not been affected by either one or both of these fates.

The history of science is replete with discarded and amended theories. Those that have been amended so often as to lose their original identity become like the proverbial pair of pants with more patch than pants. When an involved "patching process" raises serious doubt regarding the validity of the basic concept involved, theories are sometimes abandoned entirely. Often a theory seems so well-grounded that it is unchallenged for generations, only to be upset by the uncovering of new data inconsistent with the old. Neither hypothesis, theory, nor law is in the same realm as absolute truth. All three rest upon a perennially shaky foundation, and all are vulnerable to uncomfortable facts.[3]

As Christians we believe that only God can know the universe as it *really is*. We are limited by our senses and our minds, and we know the universe only as it *appears* to us. In science we do not believe in generalizations because we know them to be *true;* we believe in them only because they are *credible* to us. Several competing explanations for the same phenomenon may be equally attractive, and often none of them can be proved false. Who can say which, if any, reflects reality? Usually we apply the principle of logic called "Ockham's razor" and accept the simplest explanation, but for all we know this may not be the best answer. And even when no alternative explanation exists, does that mean that no alternative is possible? Thus we are forever uncertain in our

---

3. An interesting and humorous example concerns one investigator who persuaded a slime mold organism to crawl through a pinhole and hang threadlike from it. This thread of protoplasm twisted in a clockwise direction nineteen times. The experimenter felt he was on the track of a fundamental biological law. Unfortunately, on the twentieth trial, the slime mold twisted in a counterclockwise direction!

understanding of the universe; our most assured conclusions are still tentative if we depend only on our own rational faculties.

Truth as God sees it has been revealed in the pages of Scripture, and that revelation is therefore more certainly true than any mere human rationalism. For the creationist, revealed truth controls his view of the universe to at least as great a degree as anything that has been advanced using the scientific method.

The purpose of this excursus has been to show that no scientific statement is unassailable or final. The theory of evolution, like other theories, depends on the interpretation of observations. Because of its basic nature, it is subject to experimental test or confirmation only in a limited sense.

Evolutionists often differentiate between what they consider the "fact" of evolution and the "theories" of evolution. The fact supposedly consists of observed changes in animal and plant fossils over a period of time, whereas theories of evolution attempt to explain how the changes have occurred. The theories deal with mechanisms, such as natural selection and genetics. Bearing this distinction in mind, we shall see that reliable conclusions are difficult to draw from the fossil record, or from any other kind of evidence. There seems to be little justification for the popular practice of presenting unrestricted evolution as fact or law, because it cannot be proved as such.

A final word is in order for both creationists and evolutionists. The most important part of science is not its method, but the attitude of those who practice it. The scientific attitude may be described as one of honesty and open-minded skepticism—toward one's own views, as well as toward the views of others. Such balance has often been notably absent from the attitudes of evolutionists, who in their strident advocacy and bias sometimes sound like the worst of the theologians they claim to despise.[4]

But it is also extremely important that creationists, who claim to represent biblical truth and the Lord Jesus Christ, not lose sight of their obligation to treat the opposition fairly. Let us be both cautious and humble in presenting *our* "facts" when they go beyond the bounds of Scripture. How sad that even Christians are often shoddy in scholarship, not checking out facts but merely passing them on in the form of misinformation. In some cases they even create or suppress data in order to support their position most

---

4. Here is an example: In *The Monkey Business*, by Niles Eldredge, one finds the statement (p. 83) "A relatively small number of creation scientists have produced the vast bulk of the articles and books that have appeared. *None of them have contributed a single article to any reputable scientific journal*" (italics added). This statement is an egregious falsehood, as anyone who wishes to consult the caption of Figure 3.1 in this book can see for himself.

favorably. If creationists are to show themselves conspicuously superior to evolutionists, let it first be in the areas of enlightenment, decency, and courtesy. Second Corinthians 8:20-21 states this principle well: "Taking precaution that no one should discredit us . . . for we have regard for what is honorable, not only in the sight of the Lord, but also in the sight of men."

2

REASONS FOR SIMILARITIES

SIMILARITY AND ANCESTRY

Macroevolution is the form of evolution usually taught in high schools, secular colleges, and universities today.[1] It is what the British scholar Kerkut calls "the general theory of evolution." It asserts that nonliving substance gave rise to the first living material, which subsequently reproduced and diversified to produce all extinct and extant organisms. Most of the remainder of this book is devoted to a brief discussion and critical evaluation of that teaching.

The arguments for macroevolution generally fall into two somewhat overlapping categories: *historical* and *comparative.* In the historical arguments attempts are made to show from the fossil record that major groups of animals had ancestors in common or were related in some way. Comparative arguments are concerned with similarities of anatomy, physiology, development, biochemistry, and behavior. Comparative arguments depend on the assumption that similarities—at least those that are taken to be basic similarities—among animals or plants indicate common ancestry.

When comparing parts of organisms biologists commonly speak of *homologous* organs, meaning that the particular structures have similar development, adult structure, and attachments. For instance, the wing of a bird bears a homologous likeness to the

---

1. The term *megaevolution* is used by some to designate evolution of the largest categories of organisms, and the term *macroevolution* to refer to somewhat smaller categories. We, however, prefer to use the term *macroevolution* in its earlier sense to refer to all the so-called large changes and to distinguish it only from *microevolution,* which refers to small changes that are really not evolutionary at all in the usual sense of the word. In this book we make one exception to our general policy and, instead of using the term *microevolution,* we generally use *diversification,* which denotes small changes, namely those that produced the multiformity of living things from the relative uniformity of the original creation.

forelimb of a cat, or even a frog. As long as homology can be judged by objective criteria, it is a valid concept. However, homology is often defined with reference to (1) common ancestry or (2) as the opposite of analogy, both of which practices are at best highly subjective. How can one establish the common ancestry of two often dissimilar structures?

Analogy refers to a condition of similar function and should not be thought of as the opposite of homology. One can easily consider the wing of a bird and that of an insect as analogous. They are not homologous, however, for they are profoundly different in embryonic origin. Yet structures can be *both* homologous *and* analogous, as in the case of the bat wing and bird wing. If things can be both analogous and homologous, the two concepts cannot be opposite and cannot be defined as negatives of one another. In fact, the concept of homology is an extremely vague and subjective one, yet it is used as evidence for evolution. If organisms have homologous structures, so runs the argument, they are related. However, we must emphasize that the fundamental assumption that similarity indicates common ancestry is *not* an established fact, and indeed, even evolutionists use it only with great restrictions. For example, more similarities exist among a raccoon, fox, dog, and wolf than between any of these and a cat. However, just because animals can be sorted into categories does not necessarily indicate that the animals were of common descent. A hyena appears to be quite doglike, but on the basis of its teeth it generally is considered related to the civets, a group more like the cats. Such facts present no problem for the creationist, but the evolutionist must explain them in terms of his theory. The concepts of *convergence* and *mimicry* have been the major explanations attempted.

Convergence refers to the resemblance of two animals of separate ancestry that have adapted to comparable habitats. For example, evolutionists do not regard the pouched animals of Australia as closely related to the mammals of the rest of the world, but as closely parallel to them in form and habits. Included among the Australian animals believed to show convergence are marsupial "mice," "wolves," and "moles." The nature of the complication or contradiction introduced by the existence of such creatures is this: How can an evolutionist be certain that supposedly common characteristics, which he takes to be evidence of common ancestry, are not in fact examples of convergence? This is a more serious internal difficulty in the theory of evolution than is generally realized.

The mammal-like reptiles serve as another case in point.

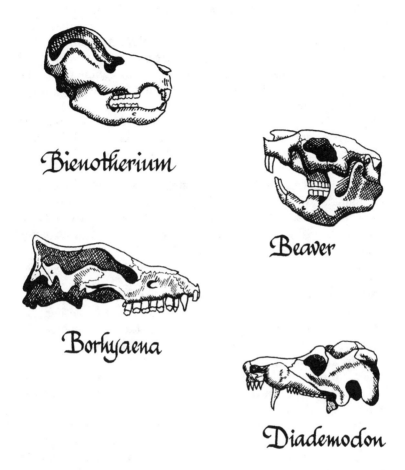

Figure 2.1 Similar adaptations in mammal-like reptiles and mammals. *Bienotherium* is an extinct mammal-like reptile that bears some resemblance to the modern beaver. *Diademodon* is also an extinct mammal-like reptile with a strong resemblance to carnivorous mammals such as *Borhyaena*, an extinct predatory marsupial. Despite these resemblances, evolutionists do not consider any of these forms closely related.

Frequently these extinct creatures resemble mammals in astonishing detail, yet for one reason or another the majority of them are not considered by paleontologists to be ancestral to mammals. From Figure 2.1 it is possible to distinguish clearly the rodentlike fossil *Bienotherium* from the modern beaver, even though they share many of the same structural features, such as the massive coronoid process of the jaw, grinding molar teeth, heavy cutting incisors, and even a small hump in the posterior ventral border of the eye socket. The fossil *Diademodon* also shares many characteristics with the extinct marsupial mammal *Borhyaena*. Points of resemblance are the sharp tearing incisors, the space (diastema) between those incisors and the heavy stabbing canine teeth, the posterior grinding molars, and a general shape that is characteristic of carnivores.

Similarities among those animals are believed to have resulted from convergence rather than genetic relationship only because the overall differences (or certain differences arbitrarily regarded as being of paramount importance) are as marked or more marked than the similarities. From those differences it is concluded that the animals are not closely related, but if the differences were minor, anatomists would suppose that they shared a proximate common ancestry. Future studies may demonstrate that many animals now thought to be closely related share common characteristics not because of relationship but rather because of convergence.

Mimicry is similar to convergence in that it involves the close, superficial resemblance of animals unrelated to one another. For instance, certain kinds of flies are marked so that they superficially resemble bees. Evolutionists believe such markings and color patterns are protective because predators would be less likely to molest those possessing them. Thus two animals that are unrelated, or at best distantly related, could show resemblance because of mimicry. Mimicry is also believed to arise when it is to a predator's advantage to resemble its prey, like a wolf in sheep's clothing, or when two noxious animals mimic one another. In this last instance, it is believed to be to the mutual advantage of both co-mimics to warn their enemies of their noxious traits.

Even though evolutionists themselves have occasionally pointed out the questionable nature of assuming close relationship because of similarity, there always has been a tendency toward such deduction. In fact, today virtually all comparative studies of physiology, biochemistry, embryology, and behavior proceed on the same questionable assumption: that present similarity indicates common ancestry.

Is there an alternative? Surely. Similarities may exist because of a common creative plan or design, according to which organisms were created in certain basic groups. At one time, this position was almost universally held by biologists. The position, however, does not imply that each and every species or subspecies of organism was created in precisely its present form, but that any changes have been minor, so that the originally created organisms would be recognizable to us as essentially the same kinds of plants and animals extant today.

Evolutionists have pointed out that certain structures often found in organisms seem to have no function. Why would a Creator include a functionless organ in an animal's body? These *vestigial structures* (as they are called) may be distinguished from *rudimentary* structures such as nipples in male primates that normally do not develop but which do, of course, function fully in females. (If male nipples really were vestigial, they would indicate that *Australopithecus* nursed *his* young!) The presence of so-called vestigial organs is supposed to indicate that the animal possessing them is descended from an ancestor in which the organs were useful. Evolution is supposed to proceed like a computer programmer trainee who needs a program to prepare a book index, for example, but only has one for maintenance of a mailing list. He can modify the program to serve his purposes, but now it contains many superfluous features, such as zip code sorting, that are useless. For the time being, though, the trainee lets these vestigial features stand, even though they do take up some computer memory space. The important thing is that it works, and as a result he will not get fired!

Blind cave fish with remnants of eyes and flies with a hereditary stubby, shriveled wing condition appear to have true vestigial organs. These and similar degenerations apparently have indeed resulted from typically disadvantageous mutations. However, they do not represent actual disadvantages as long as the organisms are in protective or restricted environments where they need not compete with more fully endowed organisms. When hereditary changes are small enough to permit survival and reproduction, vestiges may remain. However, these vestigial structures at best are indicative of changes within limits; they are usually degenerative changes within a species. Many may not be vestiges at all, because they may not be genuinely homologous with their supposed functional ancestral structures.

A better name for some of these supposedly vestigial organs of which evolutionists make so much would be "organs of unknown function." The list of human structures thought to be vestigial has shrunk greatly in recent years. For example, the thyroid gland, thymus, tonsils, and appendix were all regarded as vestigial and of no use to the modern human being. Now all have been shown to be vital, or at least useful (when healthy), to the person possessing them. The thyroid gland releases important hormones; the thymus appears to be important during early life for normal development of the body's protective cells (lymphocytes); and the tonsils and probably the appendix function in further protecting the body against disease. Even the coccyx, the supposed remnant of a prehensile tail, anchors several muscles. It may not be vital, but it is definitely useful.

Telism

My daughter was playing with her pet rat one day when a question occurred to her. "Daddy," she said, "why does a rat have scales on its tail?"

"You know perfectly well," I replied. "The reptiles that were

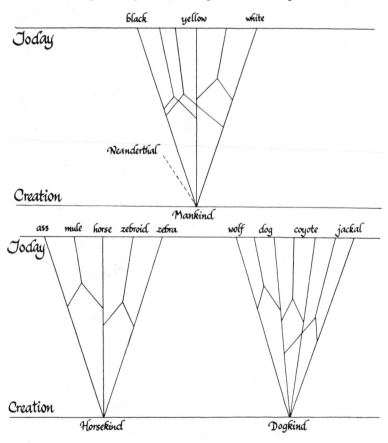

Figure 2.2 Possible diversification of some modern varieties of organisms from their ancestral created "kinds." Reconstruction of these kinds is an important unfinished task of creation study.

ancestral to rats and all other mammals had scales on their tails as well as on the rest of their bodies. Because there was no particular disadvantage to having them, they persisted in rats to this day."

"Quit putting me on, Daddy. I know you don't believe that!"

You cannot win, it seems. But it is true that one is hard put to discern the reason for the manifold adaptations that organisms possess. What I should have said to my daughter (and eventually did say) was that God had put the scales there for reasons He knew to be perfectly good ones but which may take us a lot of research to discover, since He has not told us what they are. Still, the fact was that I could not explain the presence of those scales, whereas an evolutionist can—or thinks he can.

To be sure, it is better to advance no explanation than the wrong one. But if we were not motivated to try, no explanations would ever be advanced, and science would come to a halt. Thus a great part of the merit of a theory or model is its *heuristic power*—its ability to suggest hypotheses and stimulate the formulation of problems to be attacked. Which has greater heuristic power, evolution or creationism? One would certainly think the answer to be evolution, in view of the voluminous scientific literature that deals with the concept. As Theodosius Dobzhansky used to say, "Nothing in biology makes sense without evolution." Yet if one casts his eye down the table of contents in a typical biology textbook, he will see many chapters that could have been written without reference to evolution—except, of course, those dealing with evolution itself. The major concepts of biology could have been formulated without the aid of evolution. In practical terms, evolution is largely irrelevant even to life science.

The design features that fit organisms to their environment are called *adaptations*. For the evolutionist, those adaptations originated accidentally (although natural selection preserved them once they did come into existence). Evolution is not a conscious force with a will and a plan to fulfill. Therefore, the assumption that an adaptation has a purpose (called *telism* from the Greek word *telos*, which means "a goal, an end") is foreign to evolutionary thinking. There is little that is more subject to invective and anathema in conventional biology than telism.

The attitude is understandable. It could be considered arrogant to assume knowledge of a design feature's purpose in an organism, even if it had a purpose. Yet the creationist lacks the option (open to the evolutionist) of assuming *purposelessness*. Human curiosity being what it is, the creationist will be motivated to inquire concerning the purpose of the universe and all its features. The purpose for most things will not be found. What we do find may, nonetheless, be sufficient justification for the endeavor. Our example is no less than Sir Isaac Newton.

It is not easy to discover where Newton stood theologically, but it is clear from his writings that he believed the Bible, however he may have interpreted it. With this attitude he approached the universe, assuming by faith that it had meaning and logic. God, for Newton, was a mathematician and a logician. His handiwork could not be haphazard. Therefore, a mathematician might hope to discover God's laws by careful study and deep thought.

The tail of a rat may seem a long jump from Newton and the grand principles he discovered, but the two are related. The evolutionist might speculate on the adaptive significance of the scales and wonder if they constitute an advantage. He may even design a research program to investigate the question. Then again, he may not, because the scales might have no adaptive significance whatever. But for the creationist they *must* have an adaptive significance; he has no choice in the matter. If the creationist is inclined and trained to do research, he may confidently approach the question of what use those scales are to the rat because he, like Newton, trusts the Creator's purposes. Creationism is both telic and heuristic, or it ought to be.

It was Sir Isaac Newton who stated that, even in the absence of all other evidence, the existence of the human thumb alone would convince him of the existence of God. This is an example of the so-called argument from design, which was elevated almost to a system in the works of such scholars as Thomas Aquinas, John Ray, and Archdeacon William Paley. Arguments such as theirs, typified by the famous Bridgewater Treatises, were required reading until recently in some of the most prestigious British universities. Yet those arguments were not original with the theologians. The argument from design comes from the Bible itself. The apostle Paul saw that design. "For since the creation of the world His invisible attributes, His eternal power and divine nature, have been clearly seen, being understood through what has been made" (Rom. 1:20). Long before that, David wrote in Psalm 19, "The heavens are telling of the glory of God; and [the firmament] is declaring the work of His hands" (v. 1).

In what little time may remain to us, creationists should devise and pursue research programs designed to discover the adaptive significance (the why) of some of the many yet-mysterious features of organic design. How appropriate it would be if a creationist were the first biologist in history to demonstrate conclusively the function of the appendix.

REPRODUCTION AND SURVIVAL

A fair definition of Darwinian evolution could be, "The systematic elimination of some randomly occurring but inheritable variants by environmental forces, and the promotion of other variants by environmental factors resulting in semipermanent novelties." Although Darwin did not use these words, he nevertheless believed that some organisms would be eliminated from life by the multitude of hazards existing in changing habitats. Other organisms better fitted by heredity and experience for survival would do well. These latter would produce relatively more descendants, and their kind eventually would predominate in the population. Notice that the crucial concept is not just the survival of the fittest individuals but also their *superior reproduction* in comparison to other organisms. Without this reproductive advantage mere survival would make no lasting difference. The fittest might not always appear superior to us. The only judge of superiority would be the blind hand of the natural environment, which would give such individuals a selective advantage. This doctrine was called *natural selection.*

Imagine a board in which a variety of holes is punched of different sizes and shapes. If we pile blocks of assorted shapes on this board, only those that fit the niches in the board will remain on it when it is tilted. Again, we might compare natural selection to a sieve. Only particles of a certain size will be retained by the sieve; others will fall through. The environment exercises a selective effect upon the population of organisms. Those best adapted to the environment will fare best in the competition of life. Ultimately they will predominate, and the entire number of such organisms will be adapted to its habitat.

Darwin was unable to explain the origin of variations. He devised a generalization to account for their origin that resembled, oddly enough, certain aspects of the theory of Lamarck involving inheritance of acquired adaptations. Darwin's hypothesis was called *pangenesis.* According to it an organ affected by the environment would respond by giving off particles that he called *gemmules.* These particles supposedly helped determine hereditary characteristics. The environment would affect an organ; the organ would give off gemmules; the gemmules would move to the sex organs where they would affect the cells. The then-current blending theory of inheritance would have been of little help to Darwin. If offspring have traits that resemble a blend of those of their parents, any new traits would quickly blend into the genetic landscape and be lost, natural selection notwithstanding!

It has been remarked that Darwin would have benefited immensely from a meeting with the Austrian monk Gregor Mendel. That brilliant scientist (who was a creationist) was the discoverer of genetic principles bearing his name, some of which we will discuss in Chapter 6. Mendel established the particulate theory of genetics in which hereditary units in reproductive cells of the organism determine characteristics of the offspring. Results of his research helped overthrow the "blending" theory of inheritance, in which it was assumed that offspring had characteristics intermediate between themselves and those of the parents. Mendel did not, however, ascertain the mechanism by which inheritance particles (commonly called *genes*[2]) could be altered. This was not discovered until recent times.

Now it is believed that genes (and chromosomes) can change suddenly, or *mutate*, giving their possessor characteristics not found in its parents or other ancestors. As will be discussed in more detail in Chapter 5, a gene mutation involves a change in the arrangement of bases in a DNA strand, thus altering the kind of proteins it can produce. The altered proteins then serve to alter the anatomy or physiology of the organism.

Generally mutations are disadvantageous to the organism, and it is easy to see why. An organism is so delicately adjusted to its environment that any change is likely to affect it negatively. Imagine making a random change in the design of a watch. Anyone who has tried to repair one will probably appreciate that such a change is not likely to be for the better. Nevertheless, a beneficial change appears to be possible in rare instances.

It is important, however, to realize that a mutation that seems to be favorable is useful only in a narrow range of environments. A dark-colored moth is better off than a light-colored one only against a dark-colored background where it is inconspicuous. Hence a mutation is only advantageous if it brings the organism into more nearly perfect adjustment with its surroundings. If an environment is changing, a new mutation will have a better chance of being favorable than it would under static conditions.

An excellent example of favorable mutation is the resistance that insect populations often develop to insecticides. The mutation appears to be disadvantageous in a normal environment because of seemingly deleterious side effects. In an insecticide-saturated environment, however, the insecticide-resistant mutant is the only kind that has any chance of survival. It can be shown mathematically that ordinarily any advantageous mutation, however slight

---

2. In modern genetic parlance the term *cistron* is sometimes employed to mean a gene. Actually, both are imprecise concepts. Heredity is a consequence of DNA base sequence and therefore is ultimately a chemical phenomenon.

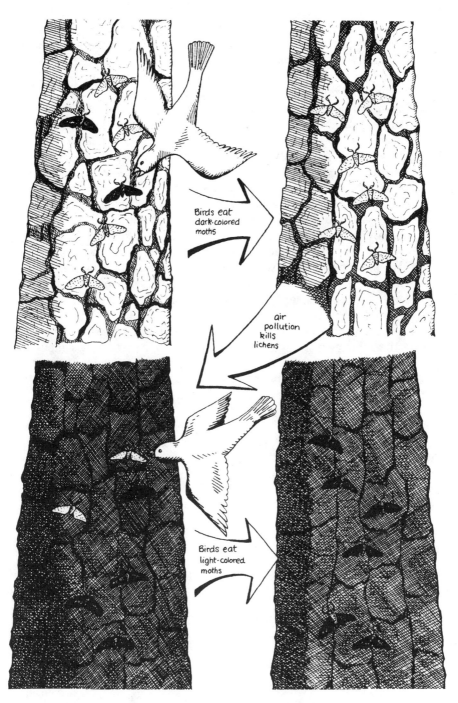

Figure 2.3 Development of industrial melanism in moths.

the advantage, will spread eventually throughout a population and dominate it. Thus, in a heavily sprayed area most mosquitoes inevitably become resistant to the insecticide employed. Conversely, if spraying is suspended for a few years this mutation will decline in frequency in the population and the mosquitoes once again will become susceptible. Alternatively, another insecticide might be used to which the population may in time also develop a resistance. A mutation makes the organism "more fit" in the evolutionary sense only when it enables the organism to survive and reproduce more satisfactorily in its *present* environment. Mutations cannot predict the future.

Populations of insects, bacteria, and other organisms have been changed through mutations inside the laboratory and out, and these changes have been noted by competent observers. It is important to realize, however, that these are only relatively minor changes in organisms and amount only to diversification. Radical changes (the changes for which evolutionary theory must account) have never been observed to occur by mutations, in the laboratory or anywhere else.

An organism is not a bundle of isolated characteristics. Any radical change in a single characteristic would have to be accompanied simultaneously by a myriad of other changes. Otherwise, the creature would be unable to survive because of internal inconsistencies that would throw it completely out of adjustment with itself and its surroundings. Yet the chances of a concert of appropriate mutations occurring together and staying together is infinitesimally small. Transitions from one major group of animals to another, if they were to occur, would have to be of such a nature. It is no surprise that they have not been observed. We venture to suggest that they have not happened.

3

COMPARATIVE ARGUMENTS

CLASSIFICATION

The branch of science known as *taxonomy* is concerned with categorizing various organisms. The species, as the name implies, is the most specific or definitive major category in modern usage. Every animal or plant belongs to a species. All members of a group considered to be a species are similar in structure and adaptations, and usually they do not breed with members of other species to produce fertile offspring. Different but "related" species belong in turn to larger categories, as the following classification of the house cat shows.

PHYLUM *Chordata*—all animals possessing at some time in their life cycle pharyngeal pouches, a notochord, and a dorsal tubular nerve cord.

SUBPHYLUM *Vertebrata*—all those animals that possess vertebrae.

CLASS *Mammalia*—all those animals that have internally regulated body temperature, possess hair, and suckle their young.

ORDER *Carnivora*—all those mammals whose teeth are adapted to a predatory mode of life, but which are not insectivores.

FAMILY *Felidae*—all those carnivora with retractile claws, lengthy tail, and a certain tooth arrangement.

GENUS *Felis*—the true cats

SPECIES *domestica*.

The system of classification in use today is a little more than two hundred years old, and taxonomists continually add new names and change organisms from one category to another. Some taxonomists are called "lumpers" because they prefer to classify organisms into larger categories, whereas the "splitters" prefer to multiply the number of smaller groupings.

The evolutionary argument from taxonomy, when reduced to its elements, states that (1) it is possible to arrange organisms in groups according to their similarities, and that (2) these similarities indicate common ancestry. Because taxonomy is a method of grouping organisms according to certain of their similarities, it is only to be expected that the organisms in them will be similar! It is no wonder that taxonomic categories are fundamentally homogenous and differ more or less from other groupings. Although it is possibly true that many organisms share a common ancestry, this cannot be proved on the basis of taxonomy itelf. Rather than indicating an evolutionary relationship, the taxonomic system merely shows that the human mind can categorize.

In fact, modern evolutionary taxonomic methods greatly undermine the taxonomic argument. If one classifies organisms on the basis of evolutionary relationships that are presupposed, how can that classification be used as evidence that the evolutionary relationships are true? The reasoning is circular.

Although taxonomic systems are man-made, they can be useful. They exist because we can easily recognize from nature that distinct categories of organisms, separated by natural gaps from other categories, do in fact exist (although any taxonomic system will always contain organisms that simply do not fit well into *any* category). Each distinct grouping had a starting point in time, and certain members have been somewhat modified by a limited number of small changes since that starting time. One of the tasks of the Christian biologist is to determine the natural categories. Although Scripture teaches that God created certain "kinds" of animals and plants, exactly what they were and how much they have changed since then are matters of speculation.

The name given the division of science dealing with the principles of taxonomy is *systematics*. This term covers not only the procedural tactics in systematically organizing and naming extinct and extant forms of life, but also the philosophical framework of the investigator. Today there are three philosophical positions held by those engaged in these studies. In the historic order of their rise, these positions are: (1) *phenetics* (present nature of organisms); (2) *phylogenetics* (evolutionary relationships of organisms); and (3) *cladistics* (branching order by which organisms have been derived from an ancestral stem).

Before the rise of recent evolutionary theories that postulate the relationship of all living things to unknown common ancestors, scientists sought to determine natural groupings of plants and animals in accordance with the organisms' present nature, without regard for common ancestors. Our present system of classification was developed by Carolus Linnaeus using this phenetic approach, and with this continued approach the system underwent the bulk of its development. (Linnaeus, incidentally, did not believe in evolution; however, he did recognize that changes had occurred from the time the original kinds were created.)

Because the present nature procedure relies upon the appearance or phenotype (rather than assumed evolution) of organisms, it is known today as the phenetic approach. This procedure (as well as others) involves considerable subjectivity in selecting and weighting features for their importance in classifying. Early taxonomists intended the phenetic method only as a framework for pigeonholing their specimens. They looked at specimens and compared them, trying to use hereditary characteristics rather than features that resulted merely from sex or varying environmental influences.

Since the advance in computer technology, beginning in the late 1950s, the qualitative aspect of taxonomic studies has yielded to a more quantitative approach. Now many investigators (popularly known as numerical taxonomists) attempt to establish taxonomic categories by making dozens of measurements of comparable structures and processing them by computer. Although almost all pheneticists are nominal evolutionists, their approach is nonevolutionary in practice.

The second position, phylogenetics, had its roots in late nineteenth- and early twentieth-century thinking. Its adherents classify not only on the basis of appearance, but also—and perhaps to them more importantly so—on the basis of presumed ancestry. Phyleticists incorporate phylogeny (or history of the organisms) into the classifying, and thus they view their taxonomic schemes as expressions of evolutionary relationships. They speak of "natural" classification of organisms, by which they mean classification in accordance with the presumed degree of genetic relationships. Their problem is that such a "natural" scheme is only as good as the presumed evolutionary relationships on which it is based.

The third position, cladistics, also involves an evolutionary approach. This methodology rose in popularity during the 1970s, and its practitioners sometimes speak patronizingly of phylogeny as the "traditional approach." Cladistics comes from the Greek word for *branch,* and the cladist is concerned with a branching order in an effort to determine sister groups among organisms. Cladists rely upon a nontraditional vocabulary that can be confusing to the uninitiated. Cladists look for "shared derived characters" (for example, the feathers on a robin and an ostrich would characterize these two species of birds as part of a sister group—in contrast to a mouse, which has hair instead of feathers). The more shared derived characters organisms possess, the more recent their common ancestry, according to the theory. In contrast to the pheneticist, the cladist does not concern himself with the overall similarities of the organisms being classified. The cladist often reaches conclusions that differ radically from those of the phyleticists—even though both supposedly draw from the same data![1]

It is our opinion that taxonomy is encumbered rather than aided by the methodology based on evolutionary presuppositions. In saying this we recognize that many evolutionists expend considerable effort to be fair, reasonable, and consistent in their research and writing, but if the foundation for their thinking is faulty, the conclusions they reach can only be correct by coincidence.

In conclusion, the phenetic procedure appears to be the most objective and most verifiable taxonomic method because its conclusions are based on data in hand, information that generally would be available to other specialists in the field. Pheneticists are under no compulsion to construct extensive evolutionary trees. In contrast, the phyleticist is plagued by uncertainties regarding ancestries, such as those pointed out by Kerkut in the case of invertebrates. The cladist has similar problems accompanying his concern about distinguishing what may or may not be shared derived characters. It seems only sensible to return to phenetic procedures and refine them, in order to classify all organisms, as far as possible, according to their creation pattern.

In fact, Classification is still arbitrary. When we were college undergraduates two kingdoms of organisms were recognized: plant and animal. Everything not considered an animal had to be some sort of plant. The result was an absurd lumping together of gardenias and bacteria, so that even the microbes inhabiting one's colon were given the odd name "intestinal flora." It became evident that it was not meaningful to classify the radically differing bacteria with plants, so a three-kingdom scheme of classification was proposed. Still later, when it was noted that organisms such as

---

1. For example, the biologist Gardiner (Zool. J. Linn. Soc. 74:207, 1982) links the birds and mammals together as "sister groups," whereas it is more usual by far for evolutionists to consider them related only through the early reptile ancestors supposedly common to both.

the plantlike protozoan *Euglena* did not fit comfortably into existing kingdoms, another kingdom was erected to accommodate such nucleated microorganisms. Today most textbooks present a five-kingdom system of taxonomy with hardly a blush, even though some organisms still do not fit well into any of the five.

It is much like the problem faced by a librarian who has been given a historical novel. Should she shelve it with history or with fiction? By custom she places it in the fiction category, but who is to say that is where it belongs "in reality"? In the last analysis the sciences of taxonomy and library classification have a lot in common. Both are practical and indispensable systems for data classification and retrieval, but neither can claim to be totally objective.

EMBRYOLOGY

The embryological approach is another variation of the comparative argument. Like other comparative arguments, it depends on the assumption that common characteristics imply common ancestry. However, in embryology we observe that these common characteristics are not static but change during the development of the organism from fertilized egg until birth or hatching.

In 1828 Karl Ernst von Baer published his hypotheses regarding embryonic resemblance. He observed the similarity of the embryos of mammals, birds, lizards, and snakes during their early stages. The younger the embryos were, the more alike they appeared to be. Even though the similarity of young embryos was based on carefully observed facts, there arose a false doctrine based on an illogical misinterpretation of some of the same facts. This doctrine is usually known today as the *biogenetic law*, which is briefly stated as "ontogeny recapitulates phylogeny."

For years this doctrine led many earnest biologists down a false trail from which some have not returned. The pseudolaw was emphasized by Darwin in 1859 and vigorously spread by Ernst Haeckel, starting with a publication in 1866. Unfortunately some of Haeckel's work involved scientific dishonesty, as is now well recognized.[2] In spite of this, certain of his diagrams have been reproduced uncritically through generations of biology textbooks to further the teaching of evolution.

The biogenetic law teaches that as an embryo develops it passes through the stages experienced by the adult organism in its long

---

2. A summary of the evidence for such a serious charge is included in an article by Wilbert H. Rusch, Jr., "Ontogeny Recapitulates Phylogeny," *Creation Research Society Annual*, June 1969, pp. 27-34.

process of evolution. If we lined up a series of early to late human embryos, for example, we could see what might be thought of as a "fish" stage, "amphibian" stage, "reptile" stage, and ultimately, a "mammal" stage. Thus, embryonic life would resemble an abbreviated moving picture that summarizes the entire history of the race, hence the explanatory term *recapitulates*.

Recapitulation studies appeared to be ideal for solving evolutionary problems, and both plant and animal materials were studied in the light of this principle. It was even used to study human social practices, with infantile and childish behavior reflecting (it was assumed) the behavior of our adult primitive ancestors. As study progressed, however, the list of exceptions became greater than the amount of supporting data for recapitulation.

The human embryo does pass through a stage resembling a fish. It does not, however, closely resemble a mature fish. The resemblance is actually vague, for there is no fishlike tail and no fins. There are, however, pharyngeal (or so-called gill) pouches in the same region where a fish will develop gills. In the human embryo (as well as in mammals, birds, and reptiles in general) these pouches are useful, for they develop into important structures such as the ear chamber, tonsils, parathyroid glands, and thymus. The human embryo never really has gills, nor is there any gill-like function in this region. The pouches never become fully patent, and therefore water could not flow through them at *any* stage of development. Cartilaginous bars separating the pouches contain blood vessels necessary for the passage of blood to the head and dorsal aorta. The pharyngeal pouches of the human embryo are similar only to those found in the *embryonic* fish.

Interestingly enough, the exact reverse of the Darwinian idea of recapitulation frequently occurs. Instead of finding in an embryo the adult stages of the supposed species ancestor, we see in the *adult* an embryonic stage of this supposed ancestor. For instance, man has a poorly developed coat of body hair compared to apes and does not have ridges over the eyes as apes have. In these traits he actually resembles a very *young* ape whose hair and brow ridges have not yet developed. This reverse of recapitulation has been found in many studies of such diverse organisms as mollusks, insects, and chordates.

Although there are some noted exceptions, most modern biologists no longer hold the recapitulation view, which was more popular fifty years ago. It is now considered safer to return to the simpler and much more objective views of von Baer, namely, that many very early embryos are similar and become more and more dissimilar as they grow older.

During growth and development each structure has its own function. Structures appear in the embryonic stage for varying lengths of time. Some stay essentially as they are; others change or disappear. But each structure plays its part in the drama of embryonic life. Structures of the pharyngeal region of man produce parts of the ears, mouth, and neck. The notochord is absent in most adult vertebrates, but if it is removed from the embryo the central nervous system will not develop normally. The first kidney (pronephros), which later disappears, affects growth of other structures that do remain and that would not develop if it were not present. Structures in embryos are not present just because supposed evolutionary ancestors had them; they are not merely useless vestiges.

In fact, one should be cautious about saying that any structure found in any stage of the life cycle (even in the adult) is vestigial—first, because its function or functions may later be discovered; and second, because it is impossible to prove that anything does *not* have a function. That is arguing from negative evidence, a classical logical fallacy. The simpler explanation is that structures are present because they have a part to play in the development of the organism, or in its adult life. Furthermore, the more similar fully developed organisms are, the more similar their embryological development could be expected to be.

Comparative embryology can be useful in classifying groups of animals. Along with adult characteristics, patterns of development are of aid in determining with what group a particular organism should be placed. In certain cases in which adult organisms have shown great differences, embryological similarities have given clues to their classification. For example, the adult of the parasitic barnacle *Sacculina* is weirdly unlike other animals. If anything, it resembles a fungus. However, its embryology is like that of other barnacles. But this case is an exception; in general, similar adults have similar developmental patterns.

Living things begin development as single cells and increase in complexity as they get older. One would expect that embryos would be more like the adult form the older they become. Four men with pieces of wood or bars of soap can start to carve a fish, turtle, dog, and cat. The longer they continue, the easier it is to tell what they are making. In two separate carvings of similar animals (such as a dog and a cat), one might be unable to differentiate until the two were almost finished.

This illustration, in fact, has a basis in embryological theory. In mathematics *stochastic variables* are of such a nature that every event that occurs limits the possibilities of the succeeding event, which in turn limits the number of possible events that may succeed *it*, and so on. A driver in California heading east could go to any number of states, but once he reached Kansas, he could only go to the states east of Kansas. In eastern Pennsylvania his immediate choices to the east would be limited to New York and New Jersey, and so on.

Similarly, an embryo begins as an undifferentiated mass of cells. In vertebrates a bit of tissue from a very young embryo can be made to develop into any adult structure characteristic of its species. Normally a bit of tissue might turn into an eye, but by surgically transplanting it to different locations in the body of the embryo, it can be made to develop into heart or kidney. Its *potencies* (potentialities) are virtually unlimited. As the embryo matures, however, the potencies become increasingly restricted. In time the eye region will be able to form nothing but eye. If the heart region and eye region had been exchanged early enough, however, the eye nerve would have developed in the transplanted heart tissue, which would by then have become not heart but eye. This is an example of stochastic development.

Evolution is also supposed to be a stochastic process. A dog could never have evolved from a bat, nor vice versa, for both are too specialized to have given rise to one another. Their potencies would have become limited by the passage of evolutionary time. However, a generalized mammal like an insectivore is thought by evolutionists to have given rise ultimately to both the dog and the bat. Evolutionary theory supposes that the common ancestors of animals were simple or generalized progenitors of more specialized forms.

Because of the stochastic nature of embryonic development, the earlier stages of embryos are generalized, and for this reason tend to resemble one another. *Coincidentally* they also tend to resemble the supposed common ancestor of the forms being compared, simply because if such an ancestor existed it would be generalized. Therefore, the nature of the proof offered by the recapitulation argument rests upon a fortuitous resemblance.

So embryos develop from simple to complex, from like to more unlike, according to the plans originally laid out by the Creator and now divinely stamped in the genes within every cell. The various parts of the embryos do their own jobs at certain stages in development, and at every point they set the scene for succeeding stages of development and trigger them. Each organism bears considerable resemblance to others of the same group, but such similarities imply a common ancestry only to the evolutionist.

Let us illustrate with an example. In addition to the differences among the DNA patterns of various genes, there are a number of observable morphological and physiological group distinctives that may be seen from the earliest embryological stages. It is true that each embryo starts as a single cell, but these cells are not all the same. There are differences, for example, in the quantity and distribution of yolk. There are also differences among the cleavage patterns of cells as they multiply.

Later in development we find differences in mesoderm and coelom formation. Mesoderm is the middle of the three major germ layers of the chordate embryo. From it such things as muscles, blood, and bones will develop. The coelom, or body cavity, always begins as a cavity within the mesoderm. Consider the formation of mesoderm in three chordates (all supposedly related to one another) and in the sea star, a member of the phylum Echinodermata to which the chordates are supposed to be related.

1. In the lancelet (amphioxus), pouches are formed in the wall of the gut. These eventually lose their connection with the gut and become hollow tubes running down the back of the embryo. They expand to provide mesoderm, and their hollow interiors constitute the coelom.

2. In the frog, the mesoderm rolls over the blastoporal lip, detaching from the endoderm and forming a plate of cells that spreads forward between outer ectoderm and inner endoderm.

3. In the chicken, wings of mesoderm flow outward from the axial region. This mesoderm appears to come from the outer layer and is not derived from the gut. Mesoderm splits internally to form a coelom.

4. In the sea star, mesoderm is first extruded into the cavity between the existing germ layers from the gut wall. Subsequently, outpocketing from the gut takes place, forming the coelom.

The above-outlined example illustrates that in embryology, as in other comparative studies, there are similarities, but consider also the magnitude of the differences. This surely does not confirm the doctrine of common ancestry. In fact, the processes are so different that some have questioned whether they even should be considered comparable.

BIOCHEMISTRY

One of the areas of comparative study that is newer than anatomy and embryology is biochemistry, developed largely by research in the twentieth century. Some biochemical methods

Rare as Hen's Teeth

In experiments reported by E. J. Kollar and C. Fisher (*Science* 207:995; 1980) epithelium from pharyngeal arches of five-day-old chick embryos was combined with mesenchyme from mandibular molars of 16- to 18-day-old mouse embryos. The combined tissues then were grafted into anterior chambers of the eyes of adult mice. The grafts were harvested after a week or more and some tooth structures were obtained. Apparently as a result of the experimental conditions the chick epithelium secreted enamel matrix proteins, which resulted from activity by genes that normally would remain quiescent during chick development.

Could those results have interesting evolutionary implications? Do they mean that as modern birds (represented by the chicken) evolved from a "reptilian" common ancestor with the mammals (represented by the mouse) they lost some of the machinery for tooth production but retained the tooth-producing genes? This is an evolutionary explanation.

Another possibility is that in the creation pattern of some or all birds, God placed in the cells the necessary genetic information for ontogenesis, because there *are* fossil birds with teeth. Because of mutation, tooth production was lost. Embryonic teeth have also been reported in a species of turtle, whereas all extant adult turtles lack teeth (just as birds do). Turtle toothlessness, then, may have resulted from loss by mutation, while some genes that formerly were involved in the very earliest development of teeth still exert a temporary effect in one aberrant species. Loss of an originally created characteristic by mutation, in other words, provides an alternative explanation, making it unnecessary to relate birds to some imagined nonavian ancestor merely on the basis of this tooth data.

involve the use of blood. Blood proteins can be compared to determine degrees of chemical similarity. These blood proteins are found in blood serum, which is derived from the clear fluid (plasma) in which the blood corpuscles are suspended. Serum is the portion of this blood fluid that does not clot. Hence if a quantity of blood is allowed to coagulate, a straw-colored liquid, the serum, eventually seeps from the clot.

Suppose we inject some human serum into the body of a rabbit. The rabbit will react to that serum and build up immunity to it. That immunity is expressed in certain proteins, primarily the proteins called gamma globulins in the blood serum of the rabbit itself. Some serum (antihuman serum) can then be obtained from the immunized rabbit. When that is mixed with human blood serum, a cloudy precipitate will form and perhaps even sink to the bottom of the vessel. If antihuman serum is mixed with a serum chemically similar to human serum, less precipitate will form during a specified period of time. If antihuman serum is mixed with a serum chemically dissimilar to human serum, a slight precipitate may form. If we add rabbit antihuman serum to the blood serum from an ape, a monkey, a cat, or a chicken, we see *less* precipitation than we saw when the immune serum reacted with the human serum. Compared with human serum in an actual experiment, percentages were as follows: ape, 69 percent of the precipitation that human serum caused; monkey, 22 percent; cat, 6 percent; chicken, 0 percent.

As one might surmise, the more alike that organisms are in their anatomy, physiology, and development, the higher are the percentages of precipitation to be expected in such tests. In other words, if a number of animals belong to the same family grouping, they show more similar percentages among themselves than they do with members of another family. Animals that are similar in other ways can usually be shown to be similar in their blood chemistry as well.

At times Christian authors have criticized those kinds of serological studies on the grounds that some results have indicated relationships radically at variance with reasonable taxonomic ideas. Those criticisms, directed principally against *early* twentieth-century serology, now are outdated because modern procedures have greatly refined the earlier methodology.

One biochemical method popular in recent years is electrophoresis. The apparatus used consists of a positive pole (anode) and a negative pole (cathode) at opposite sides of a mixture of chemical substances obtained from the organisms to be tested. Here again blood serum and extracts from various organs or tissues are commonly used. When the mixture is exposed for a given time under a given set of conditions (temperature, pH, etc.), the protein constituents move toward the anode or the cathode; or (depending on their sizes, shapes, and electrical charges), they remain at the starting position. At the end of the experiment a certain sequence of protein groups may be observed, and this pattern can be reproduced. As a rule, results obtained with a sample from one individual of a species are like those obtained from other individuals of the same kind. By comparing various electrophoretic patterns in similar organisms, one may infer their genetic relationships. Results generally agree with accepted

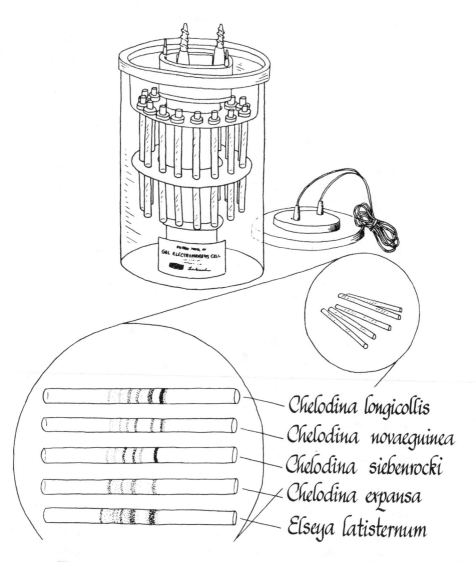

Figure 3.1 Zone electrophoresis. The names given are scientific names of some turtles from Australia and New Guinea. Blood serum from each was applied to an acetate strip that was placed in a special apparatus (a type of electrophoresis apparatus is shown above). Direct current electricity was then turned on for a period of time. Groups of proteins in the serum moved according to their charge, size, and shape so that when stained they appeared as a series of lines. The total pattern of one species may be compared with that of others, almost as one would compare fingerprints. Note that *Elseya* (saw-shelled turtles) differ from *Chelodina* (snake-necked turtles) more than they do among themselves. (Modified from a research study: Frair, W. "Serological survey of pleurodiran turtles" Comp. Biochem. Physiol. 65B:505-11; 1980.)

divisions in nature, which are based on other lines of approach, including anatomy. Various precipitation and electrophoretic studies have also proved valuable for resolving differences of opinion, which were based on differing interpretations of anatomical data.

For instance, the common American snapping turtle appears anatomically similar to the alligator snapping turtle of the lower Mississippi drainage basin. Are they as similar biochemically as they are anatomically? Yes, though their chemistries are distinguishable. Thus the two kinds of criteria lead investigators to much the same conclusions.

On the other hand, most taxonomists in the past have always considered snapping and mud turtles to be closely related. More recent electrophoretic and preciptation studies, however, suggest that snappers are actually more closely related to testudinid turtles. These results have converted some anatomists, but others hold to their former views, which shows that taxonomic conclusions based on anatomy can conflict with those based on biochemistry.

In recent years tissues and body components other than blood have also been tested, as have extracts from seeds and other parts of plants. Similar studies have been performed using proteins such as cytochrome c and even the genetic material (DNA) in the nucleus of each cell. Basically the purpose of these studies is to compare the large molecules found in corresponding structures or fluids of animals and plants. Other studies deal with the biochemical pathways traveled by chemicals in their synthesis and breakdown. By using information gained from these various experiments it is becoming easier to classify plants and animals into what may be considered their "natural" groupings. The existence of such groups does not necessarily indicate, however, that all the organisms in the group had a common ancestor.

Studies using chemicals like serum proteins are similar to studies of anatomical structures, except that in chemical research comparisons are made at the level of large molecules (macromolecules). Because the molecules themselves are invisible, they usually must be studied in group reactions. Some of the macromolecules that have been analyzed carefully for a diverse variety of organisms are the amino acid units making up chains of proteins such as insulin, cytochrome c, and hemoglobin. The results, however, often differ from what would be expected on the basis of conventional evolutionary views.

Let us consider, for instance, the amino acid makeup of the hormone insulin as it is found in various organisms.

Lower values in Table 3.1 indicate fewer differences between the

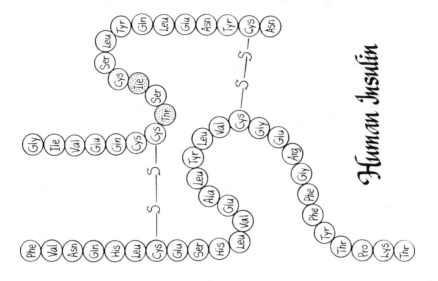

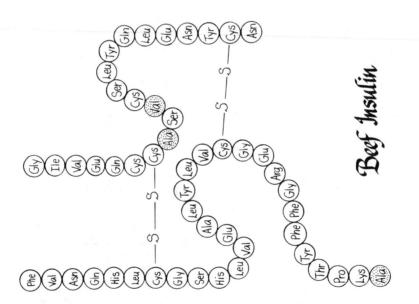

Figure 3.2 Structure of two varieties of insulin (a small protein). Each of the fifty-one circles represents one of the twenty different types of amino acids used in the synthesis of this protein. Beef insulin, which has been used by people to control their diabetes, differs from human insulin at only three positions.

Table 3.1 Number of Differences Between Insulin Molecules

	Guin. Pig	Mouse	Rabbit	Human	Chicken	Duck	Rattlesnake	Toadfish	Bonito
Guinea Pig	—	18	18	18	20	21	25	21	20
Mouse	18	—	3	4	10	10	14	19	14
Rabbit	18	3	—	1	7	7	11	17	11
Human	18	4	1	—	7	6	12	17	11
Chicken (and Turkey)	20	10	7	7	—	3	8	15	8
Duck	21	10	7	6	3	—	8	15	8
Rattlesnake	25	14	11	12	8	8	—	19	15
Toadfish	21	19	17	17	15	15	19	—	13
Bonito	20	14	11	11	8	8	15	13	—

units composing the insulin chains of organisms being compared, and higher numbers indicate greater differences between the insulin chains. Pairs having greater numbers of differences would be considered more distantly related on the basis of evolutionary assumptions. In some cases more similar organisms have the lowest values (as chicken, turkey, and duck; mouse and rabbit), but in other cases no evolutionary pattern is obvious. For example, the bonito fish has more likeness to a chicken, duck, or even a human than it has to the toadfish; and a mouse shares more in common with a chicken, rattlesnake, or even the bonito than it does with another mammal, the guinea pig.

Another protein that has commonly been used in these kinds of studies is cytochrome c. Cytochrome c is an enzyme occurring in mitochondria of all aerobic cells. One hundred four amino acids are strung together in building cytochrome c. On the basis of the number of differences of these units, the gray whale has more in common with the duck than with another mammal, the monkey; the bullfrog has more in common with the fruitfly than with the rattlesnake; and the tuna has more in common with the rabbit than with the dogfish. With other proteins there are serious evolutionary problems as well.

Many scientists have expended considerable effort constructing evolutionary diagrams on the basis of protein sequencing. Some of these diagrams appear convincing, but the similarities can be explained a lot more convincingly on the basis of design. It appears reasonable to expect similar proteins in organisms possessing considerable morphological likeness, but there are too many exceptions for the field of biochemistry to be used as serious support for evolution.

Recently immunologists and biochemists have begun to construct "molecular clocks" for the purpose of timing evolutionary changes in the proteins of certain organisms. Many of the investigations involve studies of what we consider to be diversification, but others extend beyond the probable limits of the original created groups.

A number of current investigators have raised questions about the reliability of the protein studies' calculations and the inferences drawn from them. Do the conventionally assumed times of certain organisms' divergence always agree with estimates based on quantitative differences between their proteins? Not always. But what does one expect? As with other kinds of comparative studies, "protein clock" researchers rely on the questionable assumption that similarity indicates descent from common ancestors. There appear to be good reasons for extreme caution in evaluating conclusions based on these so-called protein clocks. It is amusing to observe the arguments between the evolutionists who base their conclusions on such older indexes as comparative anatomy, and those who often come to radically differing conclusions with their "protein clock."

In summary, *molecular taxonomy* (i.e., classification based on molecular research) has not produced sufficient evidence to establish evolutionary relationships based on existing similarities. As indicated in earlier sections (particularly those on anatomy), those similarities probably result from design and can be used to determine the basic groupings found in nature.

BEHAVIOR

A newcomer to the field of comparative studies is *behavioral science*, which is sometimes also considered a branch of psychology. In behavioral studies considerable stress is placed on instincts, the inborn behavior patterns that are transferred from parent to offspring in the same way that various body structures and functions are passed on. To take one example, many birds, reptiles, and mammals scratch their heads with a hind limb. Some do so in a similar pattern. The dog rests on three legs and reaches one hind leg forward to scratch. The bird rests on one foot and lowers its two wings, assuming a tripod position like the dog, and then scratches its head with the claws of the other foot. Such similarities have been cited to support evolutionary hypotheses, especially behavioral studies of certain groups of birds. Similar behavioral patterns, however, may also be taken as evidence reflecting the pattern of creation. It is, after all, not astonishing that animals that are similar in other ways also exhibit similar behavior.

Furthermore, even evolutionists cannot be confident that similar behaviors in two genetically identical animals result from a genetic relationship. Even if evolution were true, how could we know that similar behaviors did not evolve independently? Therefore, behavioral similarities cannot very well be taken as evidence for evolution. (The subject of behavior is more fully discussed in Chapter 6.)

4

THE HISTORY OF EARTH AND ITS ORGANISMS

GEOLOGY

There are really only two philosophically defensible views of the origin and development of life. These are organic evolution and special creation.[1] Supporters of both views must accept the valid evidence, although they may differ on the *interpretation* of that evidence. In the final analysis the most concrete evidence we have is that of the fossil record, and all theories must be considered in relation to it.

Since the creation of the earth, various mechanical and chemical processes have left their marks on its crust. In the upper part of that crust are found many evidences that life existed long ago. The remnants of that early life are known as fossils, whether they are frozen mammoths, petrified material such as wood, footprints, leaf prints, or even tunnels left by worms. Dating those fossils has never been an easy task. Sometimes they are dated by the ages that have already been assigned to other organisms found in the same locality or stratum of rock. In other cases radioactive dating and (formerly) measurement of salt accumulation have been used. From our standpoint it is significant that at a certain time in the generally accepted geological calendar (popularly called the Cambrian Period), numerous fossils are found that are virtually absent from older layers of rock.[2] From a scientific standpoint

---

1. In theory, various combinations of the two are possible, but all views of origins seem to embody at least one of these approaches. Historically, organic (and for that matter, inorganic) evolution has been the only alternative to the older view of special creation. Hybrid theories have, for the most part, been proposed subsequent to the publication of *The Origin of Species.*

2. A number of very small *microfossils* have been discovered in rocks that are thought to be precambrian in age, but it appears at this time that there are no properly authenticated remains of *multicellular* organisms in precambrian sediments (except in the case of some that are so late a case could be made for considering the formations to be Cambrian).

alone it is evident that something spectacular occurred at that time. It seems at least reasonable to suggest that the abrupt change reflects some special activity of God.

Admittedly, one of the arguments for evolution that has been most difficult for Christians to deal with is the historical argument. The fossil record is very impressive; no one who has visited a great museum can deny the reality of the rich and varied forms of life that have inhabited our planet in the past. But viewed as a whole, the fossil record actually becomes one of the strongest supports for creation.

Gaps are almost always present in that record just at the point where a gradual transition from one major group of organisms to another would be expected, according to macroevolutionary theory. Some of those gaps are more striking than others. For example, the ancestry of sharks is somewhat unclear to evolutionists because of the absence of intermediate forms between them and their possible ancestors. A critical review of the published material shows a similar gap between the allegedly most primitive land tetrapods and their supposed fish ancestors.

Several other outstanding examples could be cited. One is the total lack of plausible ancestors for the extinct aquatic reptiles known as *ichthyosaurs*. In the botanical kingdom, the class Angiosperms (vascular plants with enclosed seeds that make up about 85 percent of all present plant life) seems to have made a sudden appearance, and there are no known forms with sufficient similarity to have been their direct ancestors. A similar situation exists for the class Insecta (which contains about 80 percent of all species of animal life), despite the publication of numerous unsuccessful hypotheses attempting to account for their origin.

Though examples of gaps could be multiplied, it is only fair to point out that in some cases what may appear to the creationist as a vast gulf between groups of organisms appears to the evolutionist as a trifling discontinuity. The reality of those gaps is, however, well attested by the efforts of evolutionists to account for them in theory. However many specimens are discovered and classified in definite groups, the links between those groups remain unknown.

Over a hundred years ago Darwin recognized the importance of the problem of fossil gaps. Realizing that these gaps weakened his general theory he wrote,

> This, perhaps, is the most obvious and serious objection which can be urged against the theory. The explanation lies, as I believe, in the extreme imperfection of the geological record.[3]

---

3. Charles Darwin, *The Origin of Species*, 6th ed., intro. W. R. Thompson (New York: E. P. Dutton, 1956), pp. 292-93.

If, as Darwin thought, the answer did indeed lie in the imperfection of the geological record, one would expect more thorough collecting to reduce or eliminate many of the gaps formerly thought to exist. But increased collecting over the decades has failed to eliminate these many gaps. On the whole, the discontinuities have been *emphasized* with increased collecting. There appears to be little question that the gaps are real, and it seems increasingly less likely that they will be filled.

Gaps in the fossil record are a mainstay of creationism, but evolutionists often deny that they exist at all. We possess, according to them, the most ideal transitional forms that could be imagined to bridge those gaps. And that is just the problem—how they are imagined. Too often they become rationalizations for evolution rather than genuine evidence in its favor. "It's like points on a graph," an evolutionist friend once said. "You have the fossils of both the ancestral and descendant forms. Intermediate types *had* to exist. Usually it's not hard to figure out what they would have been like."

Around the turn of the century a number of fossil hominids thought to be ancestral to humans were known to paleontology. Essentially those were what we today call Neanderthal man (now generally acknowledged to be a race of *Homo sapiens* and clearly human) and *Homo erectus*, an example of which is Java man. Those forms surely were not apes or anything like apes, so they cannot be considered transitional forms between people and apes, or between people and the apelike, hypothetical common ancestor of man and apes. The embarrassment did not go unnoticed by the creationists and other skeptics of the day. What was needed was a real missing link. Someone—we do not really know who—obligingly supplied one.

We do know who discovered that missing link. His name was Charles Dawson, an amateur fossil collector who lived in the Piltdown district of England. In 1912, in a gravel pit in the neighborhood, Dawson discovered an apparently human skull whose upper jaw was missing. The loss, however, was more than made up for by the presence of the lower jaw, which appeared to be intermediate between that of a human and an ape. A human jaw, for instance, has molar teeth that have much smaller cusps than corresponding ape teeth do. Human canine teeth, unlike the Dracula-like fangs with which so many other primates intimidate one another, are incisiform, that is, small and conical and used for ordinary biting and shearing of food. The Piltdown jaw had reduced canines and low molar cusps, very similar to those of human beings. It also had the apelike U-shaped form, rather than the V-shape of the hominid dental arcade. Additionally, it lacked a chin, not usual in modern *Homo sapiens,* but typical of both Neanderthal man and *Homo erectus.* Such a mixture of human and apelike traits was just what was needed, and Piltdown man was "scientifically" named *Eoanthropus dawsoni.* Thus canonized, he was admitted to the ranks of our ancestors where he remained for many years. The British paleontologist Smith Woodward, who was very thoroughly fooled regarding the discovery, even wrote a book about him that must now be viewed as a classic of science fiction: *The Earliest Englishman.*

At that time the first fossils of Australopithecines were being found in Africa, and as those accumulated it became evident that they made even better missing links than did Piltdown man. But if that was so, what could be done with the earliest Englishman? Many odd explanations were advanced in professional circles (the matter was largely ignored or glossed over in the popular press). The possibility of fraud, however, was only seriously investigated in the early 1950s, when it was shown that the bones had been extensively altered. The jaw was simply that of an orangutan whose teeth had been filed down. It had been stained to give the appearance of great age, to match the skull. Thus Piltdown man was dropped from the family tree of mankind.

Why then do we resurrect his ghost? Merely to show that it is not too hard to find evidence to support firmly held convictions. We do not mean even to imply that other fossil intermediates are fraudulent. What we do propose is that they may not be intermediates. Even if the evolution of man from some apelike ancestor was a fact, we cannot know that the Australopithecines or other candidates lay in the line of human descent. In fact, that is the heart of the debate about those creatures in anthropological circles. Put simply, if one cannot be sure that something *is* an intermediate form, it cannot be said that it fills the gap.

Let us view another famous intermediate in that light. Remarkable fossils were uncovered in the Door quarry of Solnhofen, Germany in 1861 and again in 1877. The limestone in which they were embedded had preserved not only the customary bones of those vertebrates but their body covering as well. The bones were those of a small dinosaur. The body covering, however, was not scales but feathers. Like the later Piltdown man, *Archaeopteryx* seemed a perfect intermediate form, but unlike Piltdown man it was no fake. There are, however, disturbing analogies between Piltdown man and *Archaeopteryx* that have come to light with careful study. Both are hodgepodges of traits found in the forms they are supposed to link, and *each trait*

E. HATCHER

Figure 4.1 *Archaeopteryx*. Commonly cited as a link between the reptiles and birds, *Archaeopteryx* was probably a small feathered dinosaur incapable of flight. We suggest that *Archaeopteryx* may be a specially created mosaic of reptilian and bird characteristics. Original painting by Ellie Hatcher.

present in essentially *fully developed* form rather than in an intermediate state. Allowing for alterations, Piltdown's jaw was that of an orangutan; *Archaeopteryx's* skull was a dinosaur skull. Moreover, Piltdown man's cranium was a *Homo sapiens* skull; *Archaeopteryx's* feathers were ordinary feathers, differing in no significant way from those of a strong flying bird such as a falcon. They were almost its only distinctively avian feature. The lack of proper and sufficient bony attachments for powerful flight muscles is enough to rule out the possibility that *Archaeopteryx* could even fly, feathers notwithstanding

Archaeopteryx is still accepted as an intermediate form, at least until something better comes along, but its nature has been rethought of late by evolutionists. Suppose, they suggest, that dinosaurs were warm-blooded (and there is good reason to think they were). A large dinosaur had a small surface area *in proportion to* its volume, but a small dinosaur had a relatively *large* surface area in proportion to its volume. Because body heat is lost through the surface of the body, the greater the proportional surface area, the more body heat is lost. That means that a small, warm-blooded animal loses body heat much faster than a large one. That loss must be compensated for either by a higher metabolic rate (burning more food to make more heat) or by insulation. Several kinds of insulation occur among warm-blooded or semiwarm-blooded animals. Bees and moths have furlike coverings, and mammals usually have fur (or, as in the case of walruses and human beings, subcutaneous fat). Birds have the best insulation of all—feathers.

There were very few small dinosaurs. Even most baby dinosaurs were surprisingly large, as far as we can tell. That may have left an ecological niche vacant in the ancient world, evolutionists speculate, one that could be filled with rabbit- or cat-sized dinosaurs if only the probably acute heat loss problem could be solved. Perhaps the solution was feathers. If there was a class of small feathered dinosaurs, perhaps *Archaeopteryx* is not directly ancestral to birds after all, but only the Jurassic equivalent of a cat or large weasel. But birds would perhaps have evolved from some other representative of *Archaeopteryx's* still largely unknown group of species.

There is a lot of speculation in all that, so perhaps we are entitled to speculate ourselves. Perhaps God created a class of small feathered dinosaurs, few of whose fossils have survived. And He also created birds. Birds have feathers; *Archaeopteryx* had feathers. What of that? Birds have beaks and so do turtles!

Granted, we have yet to hear turtles proposed as ancestors for birds. Their other anatomical features would rule them out. But the same is true of *Archaeopteryx*. Like other dinosaurs, *Archaeopteryx* had three digits on its "wing." A few modern birds, like the South American hoatzin, also have wing digits, but the hoatzin has two. In addition, there is no greater significance to the fact that *Archaeopteryx* and some of its contemporaries possessed teeth than that the platypus mammal of our day possesses a bill. We would not see it as so important if it were not so novel—if some of those toothed birds had survived to join the birds of today.

There is no reason a form like *Archaeopteryx* could not have been created specially; and there is no reason, from a purely logical point of view, that that is not as likely an explanation for its existence as the evolutionary one. Even some evolutionists do not regard *Archaeopteryx* as ancestral to modern birds, especially those who hold that birds are most closely related to crocodiles. (Those who do consider *Archaeopteryx* a reptile-bird intermediate would link it to the theropod dinosaurs.)

It is interesting that *Archaeopteryx's* status as a peculiar reptile-bird evolutionary link has been challenged by the recent discovery of the remains of another more modern bird in a rock deposit thought to be about the same age (Jurassic) as that containing *Archaeopteryx*. *Archaeopteryx* could, in fact, have been a creature on the way to extinction. Although it had some reptilian features, it also possessed feathers with anteriorly displaced main shafts. That asymmetrical feather was the same kind as that found on modern *strong* flying birds like falcons. Modern poor fliers and flightless birds possess symmetrical feathers. The feathers of *Archaeopteryx* suggest that the creature was a skillful flyer or glider, at the same time that its skeleton suggests otherwise. *Archaeopteryx* is a mosaic of characteristics almost impossible to interpret, let alone to base evolutionary theories on!

The origin of birds is shrouded in mystery, as is true for other groups. Nevertheless, it has been a tantalizing exercise for generations of budding biologists and professionals to select among potential avian (usually reptilianlike) ancestors. Those involved in these studies would do well to consider a creation alternative that relieves the investigator of the need to fit his data into a phylogenetic framework when the evidence for an evolutionary scheme is anything but compelling.

Intermediate forms are poor evidences for evolution because they imply a circular argument, as arguments for evolution tend to be. The argument usually begins with the assumption that evolution has occurred and that therefore later forms have descended from earlier ones. *If* it can be established which forms are later and which are earlier, and if, on other grounds, we can decide which forms are descended from which, *then* we can know what intermediate forms to look for. If we find something that approximates those forms, we take it to be a vindication of evolution. In this fashion we could suggest, for instance, that vertebrates have descended from something like horseshoe crabs because intermediate forms (ancient placoderm fishes) occur at about the right place in the fossil record. Ridiculous? Evidently not. It was once seriously proposed, and is still occasionally considered.

Just as Darwin predicted, creationists have urged the presence of gaps in the fossil record against evolution for more than a hundred years. There has never been a satisfactory answer to this charge, although as Darwin himself rather lamely suggested, the explanation could lie in the extreme imperfection of the fossil record. It is indeed improbable that any given organism will die under the rather rare conditions required for fossilization. When it does and is fossilized, there is an excellent chance that subsequent erosion or other destructive geological events will destroy it. Should it survive, the chances are poor that we will ever run across it, or if we do, that it will be properly described in the scientific literature. We have known of cases in which paleontologists (for unknown reasons) saved important fossils, sometimes until their deaths, without letting others so much as look at them.

On the other hand, those explanations of gaps in the record cannot apply to any really common form of life. If there are enough specimens available, at least some of them are sure to be properly entombed, fossilized, preserved, unearthed, and described. The paleontologists of the future will have no trouble finding fossilized people, dogs, cats, rats, chickens, and sparrows. Whooping cranes and snail darters will almost certainly elude them. This means there are two possible explanations for the absence of transitional forms from the fossil record; either they did not exist (and we strongly doubt they did); or they were very rare forms, possibly restricted to a small and out-of-the-way habitat.

Many fossils have been discovered since Darwin's day, but there is no sign that the gaps will be filled as many of them probably would have been if Darwin's explanation were correct. How can evolution account for them? The paleontologist George Gaylord Simpson was one of the first to attempt to deal seriously with the problem. Simpson noted that most fossil evidence for evolution was evidence for what we would call *microevolution*—slow and relatively minor changes within a species, comparable to the differences between Neanderthal and modern people. That slow or *bradytelic* evolution probably did not produce such changes as the original adaptation of vertebrates for land life or the emergence of insects from whatever ancestors they may have had. Those demand a much more rapid or *tachytelic* mode of evolution. Evolution proceeds, Simpson believed, by quantum jumps. Thus his proposal is known as *quantum evolution.*

But what kind of genetic change could produce such a quantum leap? One could imagine a gene that would produce some freakish trait like an excessively reduced pelvic girdle in whales. But the whale's life-style also requires a multitude of other adaptations in addition to prolonged submergence, sonar-based navigation, loss of body heat to the surrounding water, and so on. If these did not occur simultaneously, the ancestral whale would be no more than a hopeless monster, doomed to die (in all likelihood) even before it was weaned.

Richard Goldschmidt, a refugee from Nazi Germany and a noted biologist, advanced a novel proposal that, although it has never gained much credence among biologists, has served as the ancestor of the position taken by some modern evolutionary apologists. Although acknowledging that radical changes would usually produce hopeless monsters, Goldschmidt noted that because the history of the earth is very long, occasionally the improbable would occur and some *hopeful* monsters would be born. The first bird, he proposed, may have been hatched from a reptilian egg.

In reality, Goldschmidt was not the first to observe that radical changes can take place in a single generation. Very substantial, abrupt changes, especially in plants, can result from polyploidy and can be documented historically, mostly in the origin of new agricultural and horticultural varieties. Goldschmidt also was not the first to observe that relatively minor alterations in genes governing development can produce major changes in form or other characteristics in a single generation. Despite the lack of acceptance of *saltationism* (as Goldschmidt's proposal became known), the fact of discontinuity in the fossil record would not go away, but instead became more pronounced. This has led in recent years to the theory of *punctuated equilibrium*, proposed by Gould, Eldredge, Stanley, and other paleontologists and biologists. These researchers view evolution as consisting of extended periods of stasis, lasting in many cases for millions of years, in which species change little if at all. But these are interrupted—"punctuated"—by times of extremely rapid change. If the burst of change was very rapid or took place in isolated areas, few or none of the linking forms may have been preserved in the fossil record.

From the evolutionary viewpoint, the concept is not unreasonable, and there are some striking examples of highly aberrant forms—such as the pythons and boas from the island of Mauritius—that may have originated by punctuated equilibrium. These snakes are unique among terrestrial vertebrates in having a hinged maxillary bone in their upper jaws, an apparently major departure from the vertebrate "norm." It is just the kind of thing that could be produced by punctuated equilibrium—or by special creation.

However, the assumed mutational event leading from a solid to a hinged maxillary bone really is not a major developmental innovation; it and other reasonably credible examples put forth by punctuationalists actually fall into the category of what we have been calling diversification. Recall that even mutations producing small changes in adults are nearly all harmful; but with mutations occurring early in development so as to produce radical, major changes, the probability of successful survival is even lower.

Beyond that, what are we to make of quantum saltation? First, the punctuated equilibrium advocates have as yet been vague concerning the mechanisms that may produce it. We can think of several possibilities (such as genetic drift and the developmental gene mutations discussed above), but unless punctuationalists can imagine possibilities we cannot, such possibilities seem inadequate to account for the origin of classes and phyla. In fact, without the proposal of detailed mechanisms whereby it may operate, punctuated equilibrium is really not an explanation at all but rather a label attached to ignorance. It reminds one of the explanation advanced by a physician in the novel *Madame Bovary.* According to him, opium was able to produce sleep because of its "dormative power."

Second, punctuated equilibrium is a good example of an unfalsifiable hypothesis. Remember that a hypothesis is a proposed explanation, and that such proposals cannot be directly tested. If they suggest predictions, these can be tested and if they come true, the hypothesis is tentatively allowed to stand. But false hypotheses often suggest true predictions by coincidence. True hypotheses, however, cannot suggest false predictions. Therefore, the only way science can progress is negatively—by paring away hypotheses that have been proved false by falsifying their predictions.

That means that to be useful, a hypothesis *must be* falsifiable—that is, it must suggest predictions of what will be observed if the hypothesis is actually false. But how can one falsify punctuated equilibrium? The creationist demands transitional forms. The evolutionist admits that he does not have them, but argues that he cannot be expected to produce them because so little is known of the fossil record. But when more becomes known about the fossil record and still the transitional forms are absent, the evolutionist tells us that they could only have been produced by a process which (by its very nature) would leave no trace of itself. How is that better than belief in creation?

It is of interest that a variety of fossilized forms are nearly identical to forms living today. A few examples are coelacanth fishes, the *Sphenodon* "lizard", the opossum, metasequoia trees, the mollusk *Neopilina*, the brachiopod *Lingula*, the king or horseshoe crab *Limulus*, and certain ants. Most organisms show some variation within the fossil picture. Similar variations are apparent when fossils are compared with types living today. Certain basic groupings are found, both in the fossil record and among living organisms. These basic groupings of animals or plants possess many characteristics in common and seem to have been constructed according to a creative design, with modifications that fit each organism's mode of life in changing environments.

We wish to emphasize that the efforts to devise adequate models for spanning gaps have served principally to point out that natural groupings *do* exist. Every concept, including our own, carries particular problems with it, but we believe that our view has fewer problems than evolutionary models. Difficulties diminish when one does *not* feel impelled to span the gaps.

From our perspective we believe gaps exist because a limited number of "kinds" of organisms were created, as recorded in the book of Genesis. Those kinds were separate from other kinds and subsequently diversified to become the numerous organisms we now know either as fossils or as living forms.

A CASE FOR CATASTROPHES?

Why are rock layers and the fossils they contain found as they are? That question has caused considerable concern among creationists. Are geological layers the result of slow uniformitarian processes such as erosion and sedimentation? Or should catastrophic events be given more serious consideration? *Uniformitarianism* is the doctrine that all geological phenomena have resulted from observable processes that have operated in a uniform way. The uniformitarian believes that "the present is the key to the past," and that layers of sedimentary rocks, extensive deposits of salt and limestone, and windblown sand dunes were produced in basically the same way that similar phenomena develop today.

One example of a uniformitarian approach to geology is the so-called law of superposition. Because successive sedimentary rock strata are deposited in a regular fashion today, younger strata should lie on top of older ones. So the uppermost fossils in a column of sediment should be the youngest, and the lower ones the oldest. Unfortunately, a two-billion-year-old succession of sediments is unavailable for examination. Such events as mountain-building, continental drift, and erosion are said to have destroyed much of the record. So the total fossil history of the earth must be pieced together from fragments here and there that have been spared for our examination.

It is not easy, however, to tell where widely separated strata of equivalent age may be. Here is where a degree of circularity enters the geological reasoning. All too often the age of a stratum is inferred from the fossils it contains, but the fossils' age is established on the basis of *other* geologic formations (sometimes on a different continent), and sometimes on the basis of very haphazard studies carried out in the nineteenth or even eighteenth centuries. Faced with this problem, many geologists decide the age of a stratum by asking biologists to estimate how primitive the organisms contained in it are. So the age of the fossil determines its evolutionary position, but the fossil's evolutionary position determines its age! Uniformitarians elude this objection to their methods by recourse to "absolute" dating methods, which we will soon discuss.

For some creationists the word *uniformitarian* invokes a strong negative reaction, because most of those holding anticreationist views identify themselves as uniformitarians. Creationists usually identify themselves with the catastrophists. The latter tend to stress the importance of *non*uniformitarian events—the catastrophes—in causing major geological formations. There appears to be little doubt that fairly local catastrophes, such as volcanic eruptions and meteoric impacts, have left their impressions on the crust of the earth. But do those and possibly other events affect distant places on the globe?

Even uniformitarians may believe in past catastrophes. We have seen that some hold to the current hypothesis that the impact of a large meteor threw up a cloud of material that shaded the earth from sunlight for possibly three to five years, depriving plants of the necessary light for photosynthesis. That would have caused not only the death of all vegetation, but also of primary consumers (vegetarians) and secondary and tertiary consumers (carnivores), including various large dinosaurs. Uniformitarianism, in other words, can embody a limited catastrophism. We observe such purely natural catastrophes as meteor falls even today, they say, so it is not amazing that such events, even singular ones, may have occurred in the past. What uniformitarianism rejects is catastrophes of great magnitude or frequency; particularly those that might be considered of supernatural or miraculous origin.

Creationists generally believe that a unique great and violent flood caused major erosional patterns, strata formation, and fossil depositions in a relatively short time. If such events happened rapidly, the formations could have developed recently—perhaps thousands, rather than millions or billions of years ago. This would naturally involve a tremendous compression of the geological time scale.

Some evidence may support this. For instance, dinosaur tracks and reputedly human footprints occur together in Texas within the same Mesozoic rock, at least sixty million years older than human remains should be, according to uniformitarian views. It would be just this kind of evidence, *if it could be authenticated,* that would conclusively falsify both uniformitarianism and evolution as hypotheses. However, further studies are necessary, because although Mesozoic dinosaur bones have been substantiated there are yet no authenticated Mesozoic human skeletal remains. It is possible that the supposedly human footprints are those of other organisms, or that they resulted from erosion or even deliberate fraud, as in the case of Piltdown man. If the footprints are human, the flood model *could* conveniently account for mass burials of a variety of fossilized organisms and for other phenomena not well explained by uniformitarian geology.

For instance, a typical "flood geology" view is that fossil organisms were destroyed in a universal flood and entombed in sediment deposited by that flood. The segregation of distinct communities of fossils in separate strata is explained ecologically; a marine community may be the first to be buried by catastrophic sedimentation, followed by a swamp community, a terrestrial lowland community washed in over both, and so on.

Although catastrophism and uniformitarianism (or uniformity) are not completely exclusive of each other, and although uniformitarians do give consideration to some past catastrophes, uniformitarians generally reject the major catastrophe taught by the Bible—a great flood of major geological importance.

DATING

Most members of the scientific community believe they know how old the earth is. One might well question how, since no one has

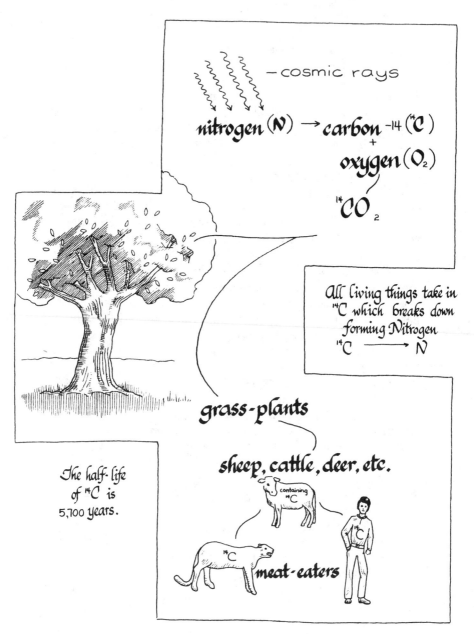

Figure 4.2 How carbon-14 is formed and becomes incorporated into living things.

lived as long as the earth, and no one would have been alive during most of the geological ages. But there is no real mystery, they say, because there are a multitude of dating methods that will give thoroughly reliable readouts of the age of almost any rock or fossil.

Most of those allegedly reliable techniques depend on the breakdown of one substance to form another at what is presumed to be a regular rate over any period of time. But one must know how much of the parent substance was originally in a rock and how much now remains, or how much of the daughter substance now exists and the rate of change from one to another. In addition, one must be sure that none of the daughter substance was originally present, and that none has entered the specimen from outside, has been leached out of the specimen by water, or has evaporated in the form of gas. If all those things can be known, then one can date the specimen with assurance.

Though not usable in paleontology because its range is too short, carbon-14 dating may serve to illustrate the principle employed for most such dating methods, some of which are regularly used in paleontology.

Cosmic rays are high-energy radiations from outer space that change nitrogen in the upper atmosphere to ^{14}C (carbon-14). ^{14}C then reacts with the oxygen also present to form $^{14}CO_2$. This differs from ordinary carbon dioxide only in that its unstable ^{14}C isotope renders it radioactive. Eventually the $^{14}CO_2$ diffuses to the lower atmosphere where it is taken up by plants in photosynthesis, becomes incorporated into their tissues, and in this way enters the food chain. Thus all living things, including humans, are slightly radioactive because of the ^{14}C they contain.

When organisms die, however, they stop eating, breathing, and (if they are plants) photosynthesizing. The ^{14}C in dead organisms gradually decays, taking about 5,730 years for half of it to turn back to nitrogen again. It becomes less and less radioactive with the passage of time. A future archaeologist who happened upon a mummified body could cremate some of it, catch the products of combustion, and measure the amount of ^{14}C still present in its remains. Thus, almost any organic relic can be dated, unless it is so old the ^{14}C is gone.

We also know (or think we know) the half-lives of a number of other naturally occurring radioactive substances. For instance, the half-life of rubidium-87 is 47 billion years; that of uranium-238 is 4 billion, 510 million years; and potassium-40 is 1 billion, 300 million years. Methods similar in principle to those employed for ^{14}C could be used to date rocks with these rubidium, uranium, and potassium isotopes, if the ideas about ^{14}C mentioned earlier could be known.

Those using such methods claim such knowledge is possible, or that at least it is possible to correct for any departures from that data. But this is difficult to believe. By what right, for instance, can one insist that radioactive decay has always proceeded at today's rates over millions or billions of years, vast time spans as far outside the experience of the human race as are the depths of intergalactic space? Furthermore, estimates of the age of rocks obtained by various methods ought to converge at about the same figure. Often they do not. Estimates of the age of the earth obtained by different modern means vary from less than two billion to as much as seven billion years.

The problem of dating is a crucial area of potential creation research. Though an ancient age for the earth might not be incompatible with the doctrine of creation, a recent origin would be incompatible with evolution. One cannot have evolution if the time allotted to it is insufficient to permit the vast changes that presumably have taken place. Also, if the fossil record is to constitute evidence for evolution, then absolute dating methods must be employed to remove the circularity in reasoning used to date those fossils. Demolishing the validity of current methods of "absolute" dating would go a long way toward discrediting the fossil record as evidence for evolution.

BIOGEOGRAPHY AND DRIFTING CONTINENTS

Biogeography is the study of the distribution of organisms. Living things are not spread haphazardly over the earth, but have a patterned distribution. The study of this pattern is used as one of the classic kinds of evidence for evolution. Why, for example, are there very few native placental animals in Australia, whereas everywhere else they are the dominant kind? The marsupials that live in Australia play ecological roles fully comparable to those of placental mammals elsewhere. There are marsupial "mice," "moles," "antelopes" (that is, kangaroos), and even extinct Australian marsupial "wolves" and "rhinoceroses." Why are they all marsupials? Is not the best explanation that they have all descended from a common marsupial ancestor?

Darwin thought he observed something very similar, though on a much smaller scale, on the Galapagos Islands. There he discovered a group of finches that had a variety of life-styles, and a variety of physical and other adaptations fitted for those life-

Figure 4.3 Diversification of Galapagos finches.

styles. Consider their beaks. They ranged from small to large and
were variously shaped, even though the birds with these diverse
features were all obviously related and shared common traits such
as color patterns. Darwin suggested that a few of those birds,
perhaps a single pair, had arrived by chance on the islands, where
under the influence of natural selection their descendants evolved
into the variety of Galapagos finches seen today. Here again,
although this may serve as an example of diversification, it is not
evolution in the usual sense because the changes were relatively
minor. What Darwin observed among Galapagos finches (and what
others have similarly observed among Hawaiian honeycreeper
birds) is not comparable to what evolutionists think happened in
Australia. Is there a Galapagos finch that is the equivalent of a
duck? An eagle? An ostrich?

For the creationist who is willing to grant God the unlimited
power He does possess, there is no reason to think that all
organisms were created in just one center. God could have created
different kinds of organisms in different places, but they would not
necessarily have remained where they were created. As they
emigrated and dispersed they could have undergone differentiation that would have fitted them better for life in the new habitats
they encountered. Moreover, could God not have chosen to create
most of the Australian fauna according to what may be called the
"marsupial" plan? He also may have done so in other places, such as
South America. The Pacific Ocean barriers would have been
enough to prevent those animals from leaving their Australian
place of origin, and also enough to prevent the invasion (until
recently) of such placental mammals as dogs, rabbits, and human
beings. Or, taking the biblical Flood into account, by chance a few
marsupial founders may have migrated to what later became
Australia and its surrounding islands. Plenty of opportunity for
creation research here.

CONTINENTAL DRIFT

In the days of Peleg, according to Genesis 10:25, the earth was
divided. If one consults two commentaries, he might find at least
three opinions of what that means! Some creationists think it
refers to continental drift.

The theory of continental drift was first proposed by Wegener in
the nineteenth century. It was very popular in the early twentieth
century, then became anathema, and has come back into vogue
since the 1970s. The theory holds that all the continents of the
earth were originally one land mass, "Pangaea." However, the

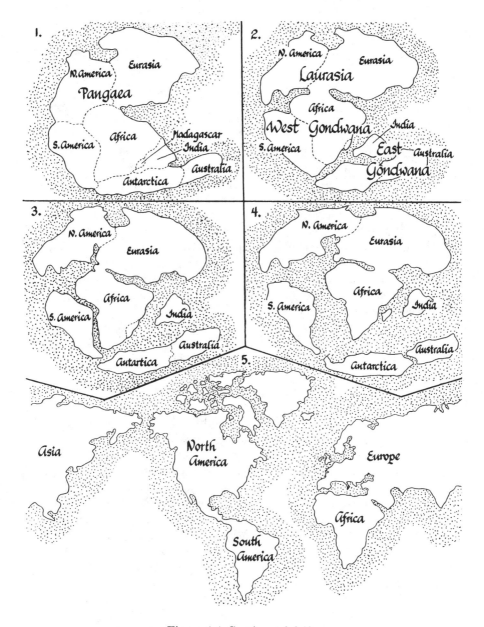

Figure 4.4 Continental drift.

crust of the earth (including that of the ocean floor) is made up of large plates that are gradually moved into the depths of the planetary interior along certain seams, which are replaced by upwelling flows of lava from other seams. The movements thus produced can tear continents apart along rifts (such as the Rift Valley of Africa) and can push them together, resulting in the piling up of such mountain ranges as the Himalayas (thought to have resulted from the collision of India with the rest of Asia).

What is the evidence for continental drift? Although it cannot be discussed in any depth here, one example of many is the distribution of the strange crocodilelike *Mesosaurus*, known from fossils occurring in the coastal areas that face one another in Brazil and South Africa. Finding these fossils in the rocks of two continents suggests that the continents were once one land mass. Among living organisms the plants of South Africa and Australia are also similar, suggesting that they were derived from one ancestral population that also occupied one land mass.

Some creationists have embraced continental drift with an enthusiasm that we hope is not ill-advised, because a problem still exists. If the usual geological time scale is accepted, continental drift would have occurred at a rate of inches per year, which is reasonable. But if the much shorter chronology consistent with biblical relevation is accepted, the rate would have had to be many miles per year to produce the present location of the continents. This would have been a sort of continuous catastrophe, with belching volcanos, earthquakes, and tidal waves. More creationist geologists are urgently needed to address these problems.

LIFE FROM OUTSIDE?

It is important to understand the distribution of life on the earth. But what about life, particularly intelligent life, that may exist elsewhere? The study of extraterrestrial life is called *exobiology*. Would-be students of it are severely handicapped by a total lack of subject matter. Contrary to much ill-conceived, sensational, and unscientific publication, there simply is not any valid, demonstrable, unambiguous evidence of intelligent extraterrestrial life. Except for our astronauts, there has surely been none on the moon, or apparently on Mars either. Of course, that still leaves the entire remainder of the universe. The evidence employed by those whom G. G. Simpson used to call "ex-biologists who are now exobiologists" consists mostly of probabilistic calculations seasoned liberally with irrational bias.

Who can know what other stars have families of planets? It has recently been proposed that almost all the stars in the universe are members of binary pairs. If this is true it would rule out the possibility of planets for almost all of them. Even if most stars have planetary systems, what right does an evolutionist have to assume that life spontaneously originated on any of them, or if it did, that it became anything more advanced than an algal mat? It is actually the creationist who has good reason to believe in intelligent nonhuman creatures. The Bible calls them angels.

Actually, there are some evolutionists who agree with these criticisms. However, some of them would rather not believe that we are the only inhabited planet in the universe. Indeed, they see us as being only one of many, all colonized from the original one. Great science fiction, but where is the evidence? Here is an example. The element molybdenum is highly important to living things in that it is necessary as a cofactor for a lot of enzymatically catalyzed biochemical reactions. But it is allegedly rare in earthly minerals. How could evolution have produced a dependence on an element rare on the earth? The need for molybdenum supposedly reflects the greater abundance of that element in the place of life's true origin—an unknown planet, perhaps?

Even granting the plausibility of all this extraterrestrial theory it is still necessary to explain how living things got from outer space to earth. If the trifling barrier of the Pacific Ocean kept the placental mammals from Australia, the airless reaches of interstellar space should suffice to keep extraterrestrial trespassers away. In the nineteenth century Svent Arrhenius thought that light pressure from the stars might propel microscopic spores in a state of suspended animation from one solar system to another. He called this proposal "panspermia," meaning roughly, "universal seed dispersal." Like cosmic dandelions, alien biospheres would seed the universe with life. Unfortunately for such theories, it is obvious to modern biologists that unprotected single-cell life could never leave a planetary atmosphere intact, much less survive an interstellar journey of millions or billions of years, suspended animation or not.

Arrhenius's modern successors believe, therefore, that the seeds of life were delivered to us by an extraterrestrial "postal service." Computer guided space probes loaded with bacteria or some similar organism were sent out by an ancient civilization and steered toward the nearest suitable star. There the individual probe was programmed to discover the planets of that star with the best potential for life, and to deliver its living cargo to them. This striking "hypothesis," as it may be loosely termed, is known as "directed panspermia." But panspermia, directed or not, does little to account for life's ultimate origin. Even in a distant galaxy of origin, life would have had to originate by creation or some kind of materialistic spontaneous generation. The odds in favor of life's spontaneous origin are so infinitesimally small that it does little good to multiply them by the billions of planets that may exist in the universe.

Even allowing for spontaneous origin, simple calculations indicate that intelligent life would spread rapidly through the universe—rapidly, that is, in comparison with a uniformitarian time scale of billions of years for the age of the universe. If life were widely seeded through the universe by our remote progenitors, we should have received visits from alien astronauts by now, cousin seedlings from other stellar gardens. Since no one but flying saucer cultists have received such visits, it seems likely that we are very much alone in the universe, or at least in our Milky Way galaxy.

5

THE NATURE OF LIFE AND ITS ORIGINS

Evolutionary studies have directed considerable attention to the nature of living things and their origins. It has proved easier to describe life than to define it! Existing definitions tend to be *operational* ones, which describe life in terms of its distinctive properties rather than in terms of what it *is*. A number of features distinguish living from nonliving material: living things require food, they grow, they reproduce, and so on. Actually, we can find nonliving models that do most of those same things, after a fashion. A car uses gasoline (food), a snowball becomes bigger (grows) as it rolls down a hill, and crystals of some substances will act as "seeds" when placed in an appropriate solution, causing many smaller crystals to begin to grow near them—a kind of reproduction.

It is even possible to construct so-called models of life— preparations that closely mimic some of the vital properties of living things. If a drop of strong glue is placed in tannic acid solution, for instance, a membrane forms around it. The membrane will swell (because of osmosis) and burst. A new membrane will then form around the extruded contents. This behavior has an interesting, though very superficial, resemblance to the form of cell reproduction called budding.

The main difference between life and nonlife appears to lie in the area of complexity, *ordered* complexity. In nature—in dust, for example, or in sea water—we find nonliving materials that contain the same common chemical elements (at least twenty-four) found in living substances. The difference lies fundamentally in the way these elements are put together—the complexity of the living material is incomparably greater.

At one time the term *protoplasm* was given to the supposedly basic and essential matter of all plant and animal cells. Today the very concept of protoplasm is outdated. What appeared "simple" and "basic" to early microscopists is now known to be an intricate system of mitochondria, ribosomes, lysosomes, endoplasmic reticulum, and so forth, interlinked with a bewildering series of coordinated chemical reactions alongside of which a digital computer appears simple.

If one compares the chemical makeup of the earth, sea, and atmosphere with the chemical makeup of living things, one finds (not surprisingly) that they contain the same elements. Some take this as evidence that life originated from the nonliving substance of the earth. A similar proposal holds that because sea water and human blood have *somewhat* the same chemical makeup, this suggests we have descended from marine organisms. But that is ridiculous. We eat plants that grow in the soil and are nourished from the elements of the earth. Therefore plants must contain the same elements (according to the law of the conservation of matter), and so must we. Moreover, these elements and the chemicals of sea water occur in radically different proportions in various living and nonliving things.

The most cogent of such arguments employs amino acids as its basic proof. All amino acids occurring naturally in living things are levorotatory,[1] which supposedly proves that all life descended from some common ancestor whose amino acids were also levorotatory.

Although some of these kinds of arguments seem to fit evolutionary views better than others, design and creation are perfectly suitable alternatives. Also, we must keep in mind that, for nutritional reasons, organisms must be biochemically compatible with the environment and with each other in order to interact ecologically. In a recent science fiction film, for instance, the hero visits an alien philosopher on a far planet and is fed by his host. Suppose that the alien meat (having come from an alien organism) was composed in part of protein containing different amino acids from those that occur in our tissues. The human astronaut might

---

1. The terms *dextrorotatory* and *levorotatory* refer to the direction—right or left—that a beam of polarized light is rotated when passed through a solution of a substance. The distinction is not trivial, for it reflects the basic molecular arrangement of the atoms in a compound. The great Louis Pasteur discovered that such optically active compounds can exist in two alternative isomeric forms that are mirror images of one another. It has since been shown that dextrorotation of light is produced by one optical isomer of such a compound, and levorotation by its enantiomorph, or mirror image. The common sugar glucose, for instance, is a dextrorotatory substance. Its enantiomorph, though sweet, cannot be metabolized by the body and may some day be employed by diabetics and others for whom ordinary sugars are harmful. A *mixture* of dextrorotatory and levorotatory amino acids is always produced in the kind of origin of life experiments by spontaneous chemical transformation that we shall soon describe. Yet modern organisms only have levorotatory enantiomers of any amino acids they may possess. It is hard (but never, seemingly, impossible!) for evolutionists to imagine how this preference for left-handedness may have come about.

simply starve. More likely, he would be poisoned, as occurs experimentally when certain analogs of normal substances are administered to organisms. Living things on our planet may bear chemical similarities to one another for reasons having little or nothing to do with evolution.

Living things consist primarily (about 99 percent) of four basic elements: oxygen, carbon, hydrogen, and nitrogen. These elements are joined to make up organic compounds: namely fats, carbohydrates, proteins, and nucleic acids, all of which are based on the element carbon. Of the organic substances, proteins are the most complex and probably play the most important part in life processes.

Building blocks of proteins are chemical units known as amino acids. There are about twenty kinds of these, and they are joined in various combinations to form proteins ranging from less than six thousand to about ten million times the weight of a hydrogen atom. Many hundreds of amino acid units are joined to form most proteins, and the complexity is so great that we know the structure of only a very few of them. Living things contain hundreds and thousands of such proteins working together.

Proteins fall into several main categories, the most important of which are the structural proteins and the enzymes. Structural proteins, as their name implies, make up part of the bodily structure of an organism. In the human body the nails, hair, and outer layers of skin are largely composed of a waterproof protein called *keratin*. Tendons, ligaments, and cartilage contain another protein, *collagen*, which serves a skeletal function in these structures and is responsible for their mechanical strength.

Even more important than the structural proteins are the enzymes that promote cellular chemical reactions. Although it is probably impossible to estimate accurately the number of chemical reactions in the metabolism of a single human cell, the simplest bacterial cells may employ between 100 and 500 distinguishable biochemical transactions, not counting the information processing mechanisms of the cell. Few or none of these reactions would take place to any great extent if the chemicals were simply mixed. Instead, the reactions are stimulated by the presence of enzyme proteins.

Most of the details of enzymatic action are available in any standard biology text. Here, it is enough to say that enzyme action depends on the ability of the enzyme (a globular protein) to form a temporary chemical compound with its substrate, the substance that it acts upon. That compound then breaks down, yielding a product and regenerating the enzyme for further use in other, similar reactions. Enzymes are specific in their action, with each kind of enzyme capable of only a small range of related actions, and in many cases, only one action.

The implication is that the life of an organism depends on its enzymes. Certain B vitamins, for instance, are needed for the proper functioning of some respiratory enzymes found in all cells. The horrific symptoms of severe vitamin B deficiency should be evidence enough of the need of functional enzymes for health and life. Again, the difference between a normally-colored person and an extreme albino may be nothing more than the inability of the albino to synthesize the pigment melanin in his or her skin. In most instances that results from the lack of the functional enzyme tyrosinase, which is needed to convert the amino acid tyrosine to melanin. From these and other facts we can infer that most of the characteristics any organism displays depend on its enzymes.

What determines the characteristics of such vital proteins as enzymes and structural proteins? Put simply, it is the kinds and sequences of the amino acids they contain. All amino acids have differing chemical properties that determine the shape and other attributes of the immensely large protein molecules they compose. Their importance can be seen in familiar genetic diseases such as sickle-cell anemia.

In sickle-cell anemia the red blood cells assume bizarre shapes in the capillaries and other areas of low oxygen tension. The oddly-shaped cells block capillaries, damaging or killing adjacent tissues. The abnormal cells are also phagocytosed (that is, removed and consumed) by special cells living in the spleen and liver at a much higher rate than with normal red blood cells. The combination of actions produces the symptoms characteristic of the disease—anemia combined with painful seizures and progressive tissue damage. Few sufferers live out a normal life span.

The pathological mechanisms of the disease can be traced to an abnormal form of the protein hemoglobin, which is the red oxygen-carrying pigment of the red cells. The abnormality of the hemoglobin is traceable in turn to a *single incorrect amino acid unit*, the only incorrect one in the hundreds that hemoglobin possesses. Other amino acid errors may not produce disease, but this one is harmful because the defect in the protein amino acid sequence is so situated in the molecule as to permit cross-linking of the hemoglobin when the red cell is in an oxygen-poor environment. That produces a gel-like mass, something like a crystal, that is capable of erratic shrinkage. The shrinkage gives rise to the abnormal shapes of the red cells, with other disease features following inexorably from that.

The formation of a crystal of sugar is determined by the physical and chemical properties of the substance itself—such features as bond angles between atoms and electrical forces between molecules. In many cases a good chemist can predict the form of a crystal if he is given the structural formula for the individual molecules of the substance. Something of the sort can also be said for proteins; their properties also depend on their chemical makeup. But the crystal of a simple substance cannot be said to require information for its manufacture. Given the proper conditions the chemical will form inevitably, and given additional conditions it will crystallize in a predictable way.

Mixing amino acids in the right proportions will not yield hemoglobin, however, or keratin, or collagen. Providing the conditions under which these amino acids will join in the right sequence to make their proteins is an immensely complex task, comparable to making a complicated product on an automatic assembly line using computer-taped instructions to direct robot machinery. In living things these instructions must be provided for each organism, and must be duplicated for every generation of that organism. In a multicellular organism hundreds of duplications may be needed to provide copies to all of its body cells. Then, when the information has been successfully copied, it must be put to use. All this is done, moreover, in each of the structures we call cells— so small that they cannot even be seen.

REPRODUCTION OF LIFE

Within the nucleus of most plant and animal cells are the DNA-containing chromosomes that are reproduced in the interphase or so-called resting stage between cell division. During most of this time, the cell engages in its normal metabolic activities. Interphase replication is necessary if the cell is to divide, because each daughter cell must possess a copy of all the DNA (genetic information) possessed by the mother cell, and the copying process must be completed before actual cell division begins.

Replication occurs in the interphase because only then is the DNA "unwound." During mitosis (cell division) the DNA is bound up into the packages known as chromosomes. In interphase, much of this DNA is in an expanded state and in intimate contact with its molecular environment. In the average cell the total length of a strand of DNA in interphase is estimated at 97 centimeters (38 inches).

BACTERIAL CELL DIVISION

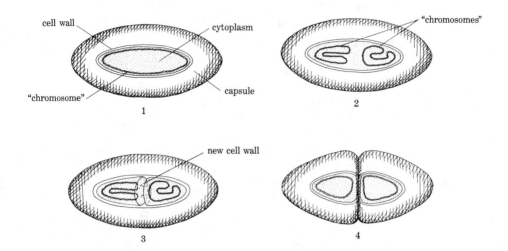

EUKARYOTE CELL DIVISION

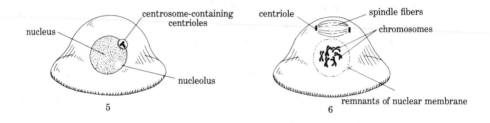

Figure 5.1 Cell division in bacteria and in higher organisms (eukaryotes). Notice the far greater elaboration and sophistication in eukaryotes, which is associated with the much greater amounts of genetic information they must handle before daughter cells can be produced.

1. The resting bacterial cell has a single loop of double-stranded DNA called the *chromosome*. It is not the same as the true chromosomes of eukaryote cells, although like them, it carries genetic information.

2. The chromosome duplicates.

3. A new cell wall grows inward, separating the two daughter cells.

4. The daughter cells sometimes remain together in a cluster or a chain.

5. The interphase stage of the life history of a eukaryote cell, such as a typical human cell. The cell carries out its normal activities until just before cell division begins. Only then is the genetic material (DNA) duplicated for distribution to the future daughter cells.

6. Early prophase. The nuclear membrane disappears and the nucleolus becomes disorganized. Chromosomes form, and centrioles move toward the poles, stretching the fibers of the spindle between them.

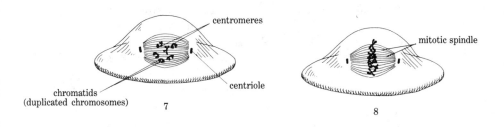

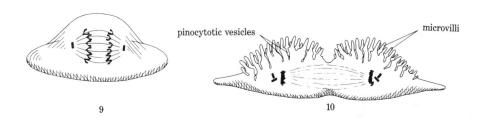

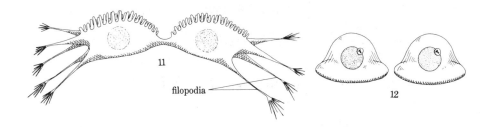

7. Early metaphase. Spindle fibers attach to the chromosome centromeres.

8. Later metaphase. Chromosomes line up at the midpoint—the equator—of the cell. Centromeres divide, permitting separation of "original" and "copy" chromosomes.

9. Anaphase. Spindle fibers contract, pulling single chromosomes toward the poles. This assures that each daughter cell has one of each kind of chromosome so that each will possess the total genetic information of the mother cell.

10. Early telophase. All the events of prophase begin to proceed in reverse. Liquid is rapidly absorbed by pinocytosis and microvilli, whose activity almost seems to make the cell surface boil. A groove forms around the equator.

11. Late telophase. Filopodia, containing contractile proteins, pull the daughter cells apart.

12. Interphase. Daughter cells resume growth and normal life activities.

DNA can be considered a polymer composed of many nucleotides linked in a long chain. Each nucleotide consists of (1) a phosphate group, (2) a pentose or five-carbon sugar (deoxyribose), and (3) an organic base. These are linked thus: phosphate-sugar-phosphate-sugar-phosphate, and so on.

There are four kinds of organic bases, arranged at right angles to the phosphate-sugar chain:

Adenine ⎫
           ⎬ Purines   Cytosine ⎫
Guanine ⎭   ⎬ Pyrimidines
                                       Thymine ⎭

They are linked to sugar units, but any base may be linked to a sugar, and they can occur in any linear order. For example,

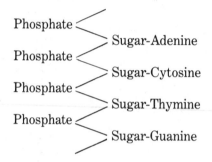

Phosphate — Sugar-Adenine
Phosphate — Sugar-Cytosine
Phosphate — Sugar-Thymine
Phosphate — Sugar-Guanine

is easily possible, but so is the configuration

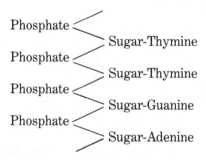

Phosphate — Sugar-Thymine
Phosphate — Sugar-Thymine
Phosphate — Sugar-Guanine
Phosphate — Sugar-Adenine

Nucleotides also can be attached to each other by their bases, which are linked through a very weak chemical bond called a hydrogen bond. For example: Adenine-H-Thymine. Adenine will pair with thymine; cytosine will pair with guanine. *These are the only possible combinations.* Thus adenine will not, for instance, pair with guanine or cytosine.

Generally two strands of DNA are linked in a double helix by means of their bases:

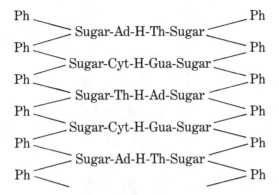

One can predict the composition of one strand if he knows the composition of the other, somewhat like the relationship between a photographic negative and its print.

In interphase the helix separates into its component strands. The hydrogen bonds break, and the strands separate like a zipper. Each strand then forms a new strand from free molecules under the control of such enzyme systems as DNA-polymerase. In each case a new double strand appears, and two double strands of identical composition are formed.

Like DNA, RNA (ribonucleic acid) has a skeleton of phosphate and a sugar (ribose), but its bases include uracil rather than thymine. In general structure, RNA and DNA are similar, although RNA molecules usually are far smaller than those of DNA.

Just as a strand of single DNA can build up a complement of itself (with the aid of the enzyme complex DNA-polymerase), a negative image or counterpart of DNA can be synthesized as RNA. The pairing of bases takes place similarly but is not quite the same because of the substitution of uracil. Thus,

Cytosine in DNA leads to an opposing Guanine in RNA
Guanine in DNA leads to an opposing Cytosine in RNA
Thymine in DNA leads to an opposing Adenine in RNA, and
Adenine in DNA leads to an opposing *Uracil* in RNA.

In cells of larger organisms, DNA occurs primarily, but not exclusively, in the nucleus, some also occurring in the mitochondria and chloroplasts. However, RNA is found in large quantities both in the nucleus and in the cytoplasm.

RNA occurs in three major forms:

1. *Ribosomal RNA (rRNA)*. Ribosomes are complex organelles made of protein and RNA. They seem to be manufactured in the nucleolus and released into the cytoplasm,

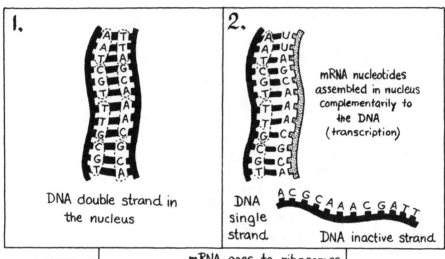

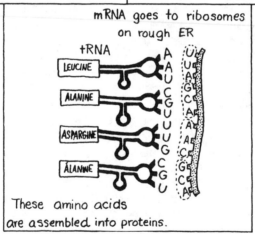

Figure 5.2 Information transfer, DNA to protein. The base sequence of one strand of DNA is complementary to that of its mate. During protein synthesis the active strand of DNA assembles a complement of mRNA. Ultimately, the mRNA produces protein with the aid of ribosomes and with tRNA. Each kind of tRNA particle bears a different amino acid, and these amino acids are assembled into a finished protein strand. The base sequence of the DNA thus ultimately determines the amino acid sequence of the finished protein.

possibly by the dissolution of the nuclear membrane during mitosis.

2. *Messenger RNA (mRNA)*. This is an unstable substance manufactured in contact with DNA. It reflects the information content of the DNA, which is "coded" in the sequence of bases that occur on the DNA strand. Messenger RNA will bear the complement of the genetic code specified on the DNA that has acted as its template.

3. *Transfer RNA (tRNA)*. This type of RNA has three free bases on one end that compose what is called an *anticodon*.

Each species of tRNA can form an association with a specific amino acid, so that by calling for one kind of tRNA with a particular trio of bases in its anticodon, one would automatically specify which one of the twenty amino acids would be associated with it. The ribosome is able to do this in conjunction with a strand of mRNA, and thus can specify the amino acid sequence of a protein.

When a strand of mRNA has been produced by the nucleus of the cell, it must encounter at least one ribosome to begin protein synthesis. Just how this strand becomes associated with the ribosome is not certain. Each ribosome is, however, composed of two main subunits, one considerably larger than the other. It seems that mRNA attaches initially to the smaller subunit and then moves past it, something like a magnetic tape passing the pickup head of a tape player or computer. However, the ribosome does not direct the action of some other piece of apparatus in accordance with the instructions on the mRNA "tape." The ribosome acts as a kind of matchmaker, insuring that wherever a trio (known technically as a *codon*) of bases occurs in the mRNA strand it becomes paired with the complementary anticodon of whatever available species of tRNA possesses that appropriate anticodon. Having ensured the lineup of an appropriate set of tRNA particles, the ribosome now acts as an enzyme, establishing the chemical bonds among the amino acids that the tRNA particles have brought with them. (See Figures 5.2 and 5.3.)

The general sequence of information transfer in the cell is: DNA → mRNA → ribosomal assembly of tRNA → amino acid bonding → protein formation. Reasoning backward, the assembly of proteins controls the life of the cell and thus the life of the organism. But the assembly of proteins is directed by the sequence of bases in the mRNA, which is determined by the sequence of bases in the original DNA. The DNA base sequence was determined by another strand of DNA in replication, and so on to the ultimate origin of living things.

If there is any biological fact that should stir one's heart to awe of

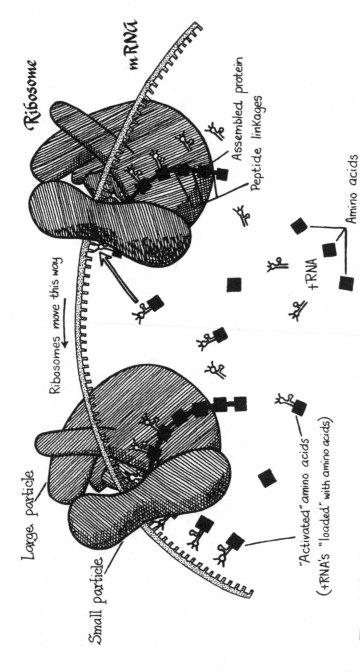

Figure 5.3 Synthesis of proteins. A strand of mRNA is surrounded by the larger (50-S) and smaller (30-S) portions of each ribosome. tRNA molecules may be seen lining up at appropriate regions of mRNA. Each tRNA carries an amino acid to the coupling region where protein molecules are assembled. To form a protein, more than fifty amino acids must be joined together.

the Creator, it is that the vast libraries of information necessary to produce and operate the incredibly complex body of a human or any other organism are contained (for the most part) in a nuclear package far too small to be seen by the unaided eye. There is no other example of miniaturization remotely comparable to this.

Any change in, deletion of, or addition of a single DNA base results in a gene mutation, and this change will be reflected as a variation in the sequence of amino acids that join to produce a protein. An organism that survives with a mutation usually possesses some defect. Even though mutations generally are disadvantageous, they may be transmitted from one generation to the next and may be found in an increasingly greater frequency within a population. It is not easy to conceive of large evolutionary changes occurring by such means, but this mechanism could account for small changes.

But how can a "small" change be distinguished from a "large" one? This problem does deserve to be acknowledged and taken seriously. There is as yet no fully satisfactory objective criteria that can be used, but an example may help. Years ago in a small park in the Bronx one could see black (melanistic) squirrels. This aberration has occurred several times in different places independently. Clearly these animals were originally derived from ordinary gray squirrels.

The melanistic squirrels probably descended from a very few progenitors who found their way into the park by chance. Also by chance, one of them was black. Although melanistic squirrels apparently have not been studied extensively, it is possible that such study would disclose a mutation in a regulatory gene. Such genes serve to limit the amount of an enzyme possessed by an organism. An incompetent regulatory gene could permit excessive amounts of melanin pigment to be deposited in the fur of these squirrels. A black squirrel, however, is still a black *squirrel*. It would take a large concert of compatible mutations occurring in the same animal to change it suddenly into something notably different from its ancestral state. Nothing like that has ever been observed.

Some have endeavored to construct phylogenetic trees based on DNA content per cell for a variety of organisms, on the basis that structurally more complex forms possessed more DNA per cell than simple forms. To some extent this has proved true, as might be expected, considering that those organisms designed to build a greater number and variety of organs would need more genetic machinery. But there are notable exceptions, as can be seen in Table 5.1. For example, man has less DNA than the frog and toad,

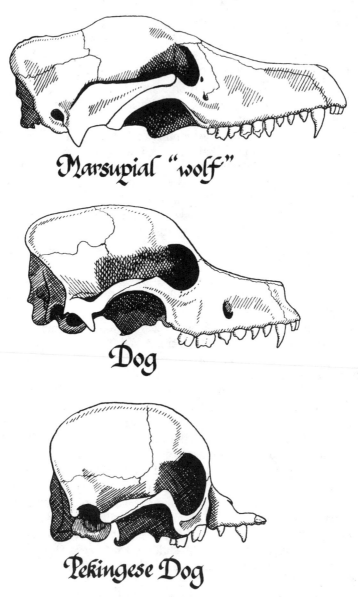

Marsupial "wolf"

Dog

Pekingese Dog

Figure 5.4 It can be difficult to draw the line between "small" and "large" differences among organisms. At first glance, the Tasmanian marsupial "wolf" may appear more similar to the standard dog than a Pekingese does, but there is no close relationship (even according to evolutionary thinking) between the dog and the "wolf." However, the Pekingese is known to have descended from the standard dog ancestors, yet by every reasonable criterion, the two dogs belong to the same species, and their seemingly profound differences are in fact superficial.

and the green turtle and fish (carp) possess more than the bird, duck, and chicken. To explain this some have suggested that structurally less complex forms may possess redundant DNA; that is, they may contain useless repetitions of some nucleotide sequences, so that the carp might simply be carrying more useless DNA baggage than the duck.

A more sophisticated approach involves base-sequence similarities. It is possible to estimate the degree of sequence similarity in the DNA of various animals by such techniques as DNA hybridization, the details of which are somewhat technical. Organisms with similar base sequences are held to be related because the sequences are similar (another example of circular reasoning). Not surprisingly, such studies often yield results quite at variance with conclusions based on, for example, anatomical similarities and differences. Which shall we believe? Perhaps both are based on questionable assumptions.

Table 5.1 Estimated amounts of DNA (in 10^{-12} gram) per haploid chromosome complement[2]

Amphiuma	84	Duck	1.3
Protopterus	50	Chicken	1.3
Frog	7.5	Sea urchin	0.90
Toad	3.7	Snail	0.67
Man	3.2	Yeast	0.07
Cattle	2.8	Colon bacteria	0.004,7
Green turtle	2.6	Bacteriophage T2	0.000,2
Carp	1.6	Bacteriophage φ X 174	0.000,003,6

It has been known for some time that the actual numbers of chromosomes do not conform to macroevolutionary patterns. For instance, man (with 46 chromosomes) is exceeded by the box turtle (50), Florida mouse (48), goldfish (94), and land snail (54). However, in studies of *diversification* the number and structure of chromosomes have been helpful. Some well-known plant groups possess multiple series of chromosome numbers, but the phenomenon is rare in animals. The occurrence of multiples of a basic chromosome number is called *polyploidy*, exemplified by the rose plant for which there are species having 14, 21, 28, 35, and 56 chromosomes. The series is known to have come from an original parent stock.

Another method that has proved useful for determining taxonomic affinity of some relatively similar organisms (certain turtles,

2. T. Dobzhansky, *Genetics of the Evolutionary Process* (New York: Columbia U., 1970), p. 17.

for example) involves comparing lengths of the ten largest chromosomes from each organism. Also valuable in diversification studies has been the pattern of dark and light bands that can be observed on each chromosome and the ratios of arm lengths (distances from centromeres to ends of chromosomes) among organisms. Observed patterns are consistent with the concept of limited change. After all, the particular DNA found in the chromosomes of any species is responsible for the characteristics of that species. Because the DNA is passed from generation to generation, succeeding generations can differ from their predecessors in only the most trivial ways.

Spontaneous Generation?

Only life produces life, and there is no scientific evidence that the appearance of life from nonliving substance (spontaneous generation) occurs today or has ever occurred. Results of experiments by such men as Redi, Pasteur, Tyndall, and a host of modern scientists have demonstrated under all sorts of conditions that life comes only from life, and a very similar form of life at that. Probably this is the best-established law in the field of biology.

However, even though the very simplest living organisms are produced by others like them, many scientists have set up experiments to determine how spontaneous generation *could* have occurred. (It is important to realize that these experiments do not necessarily tell us how it *did* occur, or whether it occurred at all!) From their results "models," or hypothetical reconstructions of conditions on the primitive earth, have been constructed to indicate how life may have come into existence. A typical model starts with an atmosphere lacking oxygen and containing a fluid composed of substances such as ammonia, water, methane, cyanate, or carbon dioxide.[3] The fluid may be experimentally subjected to heat, electric discharges, radiation, or ultraviolet light, causing the simple molecules to form larger molecules and groups of molecules.

Such experiments have produced interesting and often surprising data, but it has not been possible to synthesize anything even closely resembling a self-reproducing organism from simple substances, although a number of such substances (amino acids, for example) can be produced in this way. Indeed, many of the basic

---

3. There is considerable disagreement among evolutionists as to which mixture of gases and which energy sources are best. Thus Miller and Urey employed a highly reducing mixture of gases whereas more recently, under the influence of new geophysical theories, John Oró used a neutral atmosphere with "good" results.

chemicals used in living systems such as polypeptides, sugars, nucleotides, and adenosine triphosphate (ATP) have been synthesized. But if we compare these with a living creature (for example, a single-celled protozoan, the amoeba) the difference is comparable to comparing a few nuts and bolts with an automobile.

It appears that hurdles preventing the synthesis of a self-reproducing form of life are formidable, even with our best procedures and most sophisticated equipment. Some of the best scientists are expending great effort to surmount the barriers that face them, but so far no life has been produced either intentionally or unintentionally. If we cannot produce life intentionally, how likely is it that it could ever have been produced by accidental or undirected processes? Nevertheless, many scientists are of the opinion that life came into existence by chance or by a process akin to chance. That cannot be proved, as we also cannot ultimately prove that life came into existence by the hand of a Creator.

Obviously, we think it did. Creation is more attractive to us than spontaneous generation because it is based on God's revelation in Scripture. Those who accept spontaneous generation do so on grounds that are no more logical; in fact, *their* opinion is based on the assumption that supernatural events have never occurred. For that reason they prefer any explanation (however unreasonable) that is not supernatural to one that *is* supernatural.

It has been suggested that the relatively simple virus, which is composed only of nucleic acid and protein, might be a link between the nonliving and living worlds. But this does not appear valid because a virus does not possess reproduction or any other of the attributes of life. Outside a living cell a virus is subject to forces that eventually destroy it. Inside a cell its sole ability appears to be the supplying of information necessary for its own duplication at the expense of the cell. In other words, cells must have *preceded* viruses, not the other way around. It may be that a virus represents what was once a normal constituent of the cell, but which because of some change (mutation) escaped the cell's control mechanism while still depending on the cell for reproduction. Certain kinds of bacterial DNA (plasmids important in genetic engineering) may be such cell constituents. The viruses may also, of course, have been created in essentially their present form.

Even a crude physico-chemical description of a bacterium (virtually the simplest form of independent life known) requires three to four chapters of highly technical discussion. It is likely that a complete description, if we ever obtain the knowledge to attempt it, will require two or three books of average length. Thus, because even the most "simple" forms of life are extremely complex, we do not anticipate the synthesis of life in the foreseeable future. We accept by faith the revealed fact that God created living things. We believe God simultaneously created those crucial substances (nucleic acids, proteins, etc.) that are so intricately interdependent in all of life's processes, and that He created them already functioning in living cells.

It is a common creationist argument that macroevolution is unlikely because of the well-known second law of thermodynamics, which holds that disorder (more formally known as *entropy*) increases in closed systems. From this principle one would expect that life, if left to itself, would become disordered over a period of time. However, life is very highly ordered. If it originated spontaneously and evolved without direction it could not have attained this state of great order, the highest known example of naturally occurring order. Therefore, possibly the greatest problem an evolutionist has is to describe how—other than by supernatural means—the stuff of life could have assembled itself in the absence of genetic direction to form reproducing chemicals and cells. The natural forces that could conceivably cause the formation of a few "nuts and bolts" of living organisms would later destroy that same material 10,000 to 100,000 times as readily, according to biochemical calculations.

ORIGIN OF TRUE CELLS

Most scientists divide all organisms except viruses into two basic groups, the *prokaryotes* and *eukaryotes.* Prokaryotes are organisms (such as bacteria and blue-green algae) that do not have a definite membrane separating the nucleus from the remainder of the cellular contents. The hereditary material (DNA) can be dispersed throughout the cell and need not be concentrated, although in some of them it is more or less concentrated in a central location. Prokaryotes also lack almost all membranous organelles, such as the little powerhouses of cellular energy called *mitochondria,* and the packages of chlorophyll known as *chloroplasts,* which in higher plants are used to turn carbon dioxide and water into food in the presence of sunlight. Most of the distinctive traits of prokaryotes, in short, are negative traits: things they do *not* have. Prokaryotes manage to get along without most organelles, for the functions the latter would have in eukaryotes are instead decentralized in the prokaryote cell.

Eukaryotes (or true cells), on the other hand, have all these features—nuclear membrane, chloroplasts, mitochondria, and many other structures not found in prokaryotes. All algae, fungi,

plants, protozoa, and animals are eukaryotes, for they are composed of such cells.

The relationship between eukaryotes and prokaryotes has long
been an evolutionary puzzle, for they are so dissimilar that it is
hard to think of them as being derived either from a common
ancestor or from one another. Although the differences between
them may not seem notable to a nonbiologist, they actually are far
greater than the physical differences that separate man and ape,
or even plant and animal.

Most biologists in the past tended to believe that eukaryotes
arose from prokaryotic ancestors, essentially by becoming more
complex and efficient. More recent evolutionary theory holds that
eukaryotes arose from a cooperative union among prokaryotes of
several varieties. Since such a cooperative union (in which all
partners benefit) is known as *symbiosis*, this theory is termed the
endosymbiotic theory.

The endosymbiotic theory holds that the original ancestral
eukaryotic cell was probably ameboid, and may not have been able
to respire oxygen. It was, however, efficient in feeding. Certain
bacteria invaded this cell (they may have entered earlier as food),
took up permanent residence, and established a cooperative
relationship whereby the host cell obtained food and the bacteria
consumed it, providing chemical energy for both partners. Those
bacteria eventually evolved into the mitochondria of modern
eukaryotes. Perhaps in order to safeguard the DNA of the host cell
and prevent it from being consumed by the mitochondria, it
became necessary to provide a membrane between it and them.
Such a membrane, walling off the hereditary material of the cell's
nucleus from the mitochondria, is the nuclear membrane, said to
have developed from multiple inpocketings of the cell membrane.

That process would have produced a reasonable facsimile of a
eukaryotic cell, at least of a eukaryotic animal cell. To convert it
into a plant cell, only one more inhabitant would have been
necessary—the chloroplast. It is thought that perhaps blue-green
algae invaded a primitive eukaryotic cell and produced the ancestor of all higher plants, complete with chloroplasts.

There is some evidence for this theory, fantastic as it may seem.
Algae, including blue-green algae, do occur in symbiotic relationships with flatworms, fungi, hydra, and other organisms. Sometimes they even invade cells of these organisms as the primitive
chloroplast supposedly did. More importantly, both mitochondria
and chloroplasts do have their own DNA and possess at least some
independent genetic information, which is what one might predict
if they did not originate from the substance of the host cell itself.

Their ribosomes, too, resemble those of prokaryotes more closely than those of the cytoplasm.

This evidence, although interesting, is certainly only circumstantial. It does suggest that eukaryotes *may* have originated in this fashion, but it does not show that they did in fact do so. On the other hand, some of the most vital and important mitochondrial enzymes and respiratory pigments are produced by *nuclear*—not mitochondrial—DNA. This fact considerably weakens the case for the independent origin of these cellular organelles. Moreover, the base sequence of the mitochondrial DNA (which should resemble that of bacteria according to evolutionary concepts) is unique, resembling neither prokaryote DNA base sequences nor the sequences of the eukaryote nucleus.

We are certain that the symbiotic theory, with its problems, would never have been proposed if its originators were not impelled to believe that prokaryotes and eukaryotes were related. If they were, in fact, separately created (as we believe), one needs no difficult theories to account for their existence.

6

GENETICS AND EVOLUTION

Lying between Prague and Vienna, the town of Brünn was little more than a bucolic county seat in 1854. There, an Augustinian monastery served as a local intellectual center and something of an agricultural research station. It not only raised much of the produce for its own refectory but was also active in the development of new varieties of fruit, vegetables, and even bees. A young monk named Gregor Mendel lived and worked there. Mendel was both a talented instructor in science and mathematics and a published researcher as well. His writings, however, appearing in a small and inconsequential journal, went largely unnoticed until after his death.

In the early twentieth century, researchers would independently discover the same principles Mendel had discovered years earlier. Only after they had done so would they discover Mendel's papers and come to realize how thoroughly he had anticipated their findings. But in Mendel's day heredity was unfashionable, especially fixed heredity—for if traits were inherited without modification (as Mendel showed), how could evolution proceed?

Working with garden peas, Mendel was able to show that both parents contribute to the heredity of an offspring, although often only the contribution of one of them can be detected in their immediate descendants. To demonstrate this, Mendel took a tall variety of peas and removed the male organs from the bisexual flowers, preventing the self-pollination by which they normally reproduce. Seed could thus form only by pollination from an external source, which Mendel provided by dabbing a little pollen from a short donor onto the female parts of the tall pea plants' flowers. What would the next generation be like—tall, short, intermediate, or a mixture of each? As it happened all were tall, despite the short parent.

Two possibilities occurred to Mendel. The short trait may have been lost somehow, or it may be present in the hybrid pea plant but suppressed in its expression by the contrasting tall characteristic. Mendel settled the issue by crossing two of the hybrid offspring. In the next generation he obtained three fourths tall and one fourth short offspring, showing that the short gene, though suppressed, had persisted undetected in the first generation of pea plants following the cross.

One may think of the short trait as a kind of genetic "disease" for the pea. Notice that in the first generation of the cross this disease is present but masked. The pea plants appear normal and healthy. But put two such genetically impure individuals together and a portion of their offspring will have the trait in its pure state and will exhibit the disease. Most of the offspring will *seem* normal, however.

The explanation, now understood, is that every higher organism has two hereditary factors called *genes* that together determine one or more traits. The genes are contained in the *chromosomes*, rodlike bodies of coiled nucleic acid and protein that occur in the nuclei of the more complex cells. These chromosomes are distributed to the nuclei of all new cells by their parents, and as they travel, the genes they contain go also. When a sex cell is formed, one of each pair of chromosomes from the parent enters that cell so that one gene of each kind—and only one—enters such a cell, be it sperm or egg. If the two genes are alike there can be no question that the trait will be displayed. If they are different, and especially if one of the traits is an abnormality, only one (the normal one) will appear physically in the organism.

Ordinarily one cannot tell the carrier of the abnormal gene by casual inspection. It thus can be passed on for generations with no one suspecting its presence. But if two organisms (both seemingly normal) that have the trait should mate, some of their offspring may have that trait in its genetically pure form. Only then is it able to express itself. We call such a trait *recessive*, because it is always dominated by the normal version of the gene when the latter is present. It is worth emphasizing that most alternative forms of normal genes represent defective states (i.e., genetic diseases), whether present in plants, animals, or people.

A truly genetic disease, it is believed, usually results from a lack or inability. The normal, healthy equivalent would have that ability. Apparently, in most cases it is only necessary to have one competent gene in a pair to have the characteristic governed by that gene in its normal, healthy form. Some tests are able to detect the presence of incompetent genes in a healthy carrier, but for

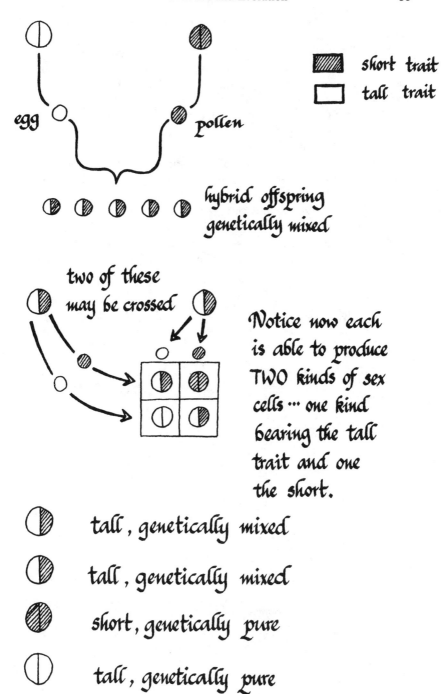

short trait

tall trait

egg

pollen

hybrid offspring
genetically mixed

two of these
may be crossed

Notice now each
is able to produce
TWO kinds of sex
cells ··· one kind
bearing the tall
trait and one
the short.

tall, genetically mixed

tall, genetically mixed

short, genetically pure

tall, genetically pure

Figure 6.1 A simple Mendelian study of inheritance in pea plants.

most genetic diseases or other recessive states such tests have not been developed.

When Mendel's principles became widely known in the early 1900s, an objection was raised. In populations as well as in individuals, it was claimed, recessive traits should be masked and dominant ones should spread throughout the population, so that the dominant traits would be ever more common with the passage of time. One critic cited the example of polydactyly—too many fingers or toes. This is one of the few known dominant genetic defects, and yet it is very rare. Most readers will never have seen such a person. How could Mendel's concept of dominance be reconciled with that fact?

Hardy and Weinberg independently pointed out that a simple algebraic calculation[1] could be used to prove that dominance by itself does not imply that a gene will become more common, that is, that it will increase in frequency. Conversely, recessiveness does

---

1. Here is a simplified version of how the Hardy-Weinberg law may be derived from Mendel's basic principles. If two genes governing the same trait (that is, allelic genes) are found in a large and freely interbreeding population, they will have two frequencies, each of which can be expressed as a decimal fraction. The total frequency of both of them together will be 100 percent, or 1. Thus if gene A has frequency p, and gene a (its allele) has the frequency q, the two $(p + q)$ must total 1.

$$\text{If } p + q = 1, \text{ then } p = 1 - q, \text{ and } q = 1 - p.$$

Since gamete combinations are determined by chance, the probability of any genetic combination in a zygote (fertilized egg) that will one day grow into an adult organism must be the product of the frequencies with which the two alleles occur in all of the gametes of all of the organisms in the population.

	$p(A)$	$q(a)$
$p(A)$	$p^2(AA)$	$pq(aA)$
$q(a)$	$pq(Aa)$	$q^2(aa)$

The totality of all these gene combinations must be 100 percent, or 1. Adding up all the frequencies of each individual combination in the table, we find

$$p^2 + 2pq + q^2 = 1.$$

That means the frequency of organisms genetically pure for gene A (AA) will be p^2, the frequency of organisms genetically pure for gene a (aa) will be q^2, and the frequency of mixed organisms (Aa) will be $2pq$, which means that such organisms can be formed by two kinds of gamete combination.

In the next generation the AA organisms will yield gametes with one A gene each. The aa organisms will produce gametes with one a gene each. The Aa organisms will produce gametes with *either* one a gene *or* one A gene each—that is, *half* the gametes from Aa parents will be A, and half a. Employing p' and q' for the new frequencies of A and a, we find

$$
\begin{aligned}
p' &= p^2 + \tfrac{1}{2}(2pq) & \qquad q' &= q^2 + \tfrac{1}{2}(2pq) \\
&= p^2 + pq & &= q^2 + pq \\
&= p^2 + p(1 - p) & &= q^2 + q(1 - q) \\
&= p^2 + p - p^2 & &= q^2 + q - q^2 \\
&= p & &= q.
\end{aligned}
$$

Since after one generation $p' = p$ and $q' = q$, it is clear that gene frequencies are not affected by dominance or recessiveness alone.

not imply that a gene will decrease in frequency. In fact, the degree of dominance of a gene will not affect its frequency in a population in the least. If gene frequencies do change, some other mechanism is responsible.

The Hardy-Weinberg principle is important not only as a defense of Mendelian genetics, but as a means of calculating genetic change within populations. It is, after all, genetic change that would produce evolution if evolution did occur. Thus, if genes change from one allele to another, a modification of the Hardy-Weinberg equation enables us to calculate the magnitude of the resulting change caused by that mutation rate. Similarly, the degree of change to be expected from a given degree of natural or artificial selection could also be estimated.

Immediately after World War II a spate of science fiction stories appeared whose theme was the great evolutionary advances that could be expected from mutations produced by radiation from nuclear warfare or nuclear power. We read of supermen with intelligence far above genius who could read minds or produce levitation. Needless to say, nothing like that has occurred or is likely to occur, no matter how much radiation finds its way into the environment. Radiation does increase the incidence of mutations, but that is simply saying that it increases the incidence of hereditary disease. There is no basis for estimates (some have actually been published) that at least 500 million useful mutations occur during the average lifetime of a species. Hardly one such generally favorable mutation is known. Increased DDT resistance in populations of flies or mosquitoes subjected to DDT spraying, for example, is known even in populations not so treated—but with far less frequency. Investigation showed this phenomenon to be caused by *selection*, not an increase in the frequency of a mutation to pesticide resistance.

We must also ask, Is pesticide resistance a truly favorable mutation? It is no doubt favorable for the sprayed insects, but not under ordinary circumstances. The most common form of DDT resistance among insects is caused by increased amounts of an enzyme that degrades DDT. That enzyme is present at far lower levels in normally susceptible insects; it apparently has an entirely different function in the normal life of the mosquito in an unsprayed environment. Some few of those mosquitoes, however, exhibit increased resistance to DDT even before being sprayed, and in them it seems that a *regulatory* gene (that ordinarily would prevent the mosquitoes from investing too much of their biochemical resources into the production of needlessly high quantities of the enzyme) is defective. With spraying, that defective strain of mosquito is the only one that can survive (or at least out-reproduce the normal ones). So this "evolutionary advance" depends on a preexisting genetic deficiency, what an evolutionist would call a preadaptation, a chance preparation of an organism against an unpredictable environmental challenge.

But again, the preceding discussion of pesticide resistance is not what is really meant by the term *evolution*—the grand unfolding and increased complexity and sophistication of life through the ages. Yet it is the only kind of evolution (if one can call it that) that can be observed in the laboratory or field today. It is surely no reason to reject creation.

7

THE ORIGIN OF BEHAVIOR

No perceptive person needs to be told that we live in a time of explosive growth in scientific research. This is also true of the biological sciences, especially in the field of molecular biology and immunology. These scientists are delving into the nature of life with the same spectacular success that accompanied the new discipline of nuclear physics when it worked out the structure of the atomic nucleus in the 1920s and 1930s. The results of both have greatly affected our lives and promise (or threaten) to change our world even more radically in the future.

But there is another discipline also undergoing remarkable development in our day: the scientific study of animal behavior. Just as molecular biology originated when chemical and physical techniques began to be applied to some basic questions of biology, so too the modern discipline of animal behavior began as a hybrid discipline. It was a synthesis of the study of organisms' behavior under natural conditions and the laboratory-oriented disciplines of experimental psychology and neurobiology. The potential of this new science is incalculable, its possible implications staggering.

The aspect of animal behavior that most concerns creationists is, of course, the attempted application of its findings to evolution. The theorist most noted in this field is probably the entomologist Edward O. Wilson, who has coined a name for the evolutionary study of animal behavior: *sociobiology*. Not all animal behaviorists would call themselves sociobiologists by any means; its tenets are exceptionally controversial even in a field long noted for generating controversy. But sociobiology is the central focus of this chapter both because of its widespread acceptance despite the controversy, and because of its profound threat to biblical Christianity.

Every organism has certain design features that fit it for life in one of our planet's many specific habitats. Other such features permit it to live the *kind* of life it leads—what we may call the "life-style" of the organism. Thus, although cockroaches and human beings both live on the earth, and (alas!) both live in houses, their design features are far different because of differences in life-style. These design features, essential if an organism is to adapt to its environment and way of life, are known as *adaptations*.

One of the first things we do in our classes is to ask the students to name some typical human adaptations. After a few false starts students generally begin to hit upon some of the more obvious adaptations—upright stance, opposable thumb, and similar physical features of the human body. Even the best students seem to run out of inspiration at that point. With prodding, someone may eventually suggest the complexity and sophistication of the human brain as a uniquely human adaptation. Although that is close to the truth, there are other animals such as porpoises and chimpanzees that have quite respectable brains. But their brains do not seem to help them adapt to anything like a human way of life.

Although one could not be a fully functioning human being without brain and hand, it is primarily the unique set of behaviors we exhibit that distinguishes us from all other organisms on the face of the earth.

BEHAVIOR AS ADAPTATION

A specific behavior can be thought of as something an organism *does*. Certain behaviors are, therefore, characteristic of a species, something that all members of that species habitually and typically do, usually without having either to be taught how to or when to do the action. Because such behavior patterns are important in preserving the life or well-being of the organism (or of the species it is a part of), each mode of behavior can be considered as much an adaptation as the thumb of a human, the wing of a bird, or the sonar system of a bat. A behavior, in other words, may be thought of as a psychic organ, and just as other organs cooperate among themselves to preserve life, so too behavior cooperates with organs and systems so that an organism may survive and successfully reproduce. What would be the point of the intricate reproductive apparatus of a female rat, for instance, if she did not nurse her young and retrieve them when they wandered from the nest? What good would a plant's roots be if they did not grow toward a source of water? How would our opposable thumbs benefit us if we did not use them to carve, to write, or to draw?

The student who considered the human brain our most important adaptation was very near the mark, because it is the brain that generates the behavior of all complex organisms. It can do this in one or both of two ways: (1) by means of a program of responses that are "hard-wired"—that is, predetermined in its basic neural structure, or (2) by means of a program the organism develops as a result of its experience—that is, by learning. Of course, this is a great oversimplification, but we will develop some reservations as we proceed.

GENETICALLY TRANSMITTED BEHAVIOR

Perhaps the most extreme examples of rigidly preprogrammed behavior are found among the insects, including the social insects. The behavioral repertoire of honeybees is no broader or more complex than that of dung beetles, but the societies that bees construct impress us far more than the antics of beetles, however sophisticated those antics may be. In the Middle Ages people believed that bees accomplished their tasks by means of intelligence comparable to our own. One medieval legend tells of a woman who secretly carried a communion wafer home from church and superstitiously placed it in her beehive, thinking it would increase the production of honey. Months later, according to the fable, she found a miniature wax chapel that the bees had built to enclose the holy sacrament.

The complexity of bee social behavior is almost sufficient to lead us to take the legend seriously, but the true basis of bee behavior was demonstrated by the Swiss investigator Rothenbuhler. Rothenbuhler became interested in what is called *sanitary behavior* among honeybees. Larval bees are subject to a contagious disease called foulbrood that kills them before adulthood. Larval bees are raised by adults in wax cells resembling those that hold honey, and when the larvae enter the pupal stage the adults seal off the mouth of each brood cell with wax. Then, after a period of some days, the newly metamorphosed young adult breaks out of the cell.

If, during the above-discussed process, the adult bees encounter a case of foulbrood, they practice a behavioral adaptation that rids the hive of the disease. Upon detecting a sealed cell with a dead larva in it, the bees open the cell and remove the corpse. If that is done properly, the disease does not spread readily to other larvae.

Some varieties of domestic bees lack sanitary behavior. Could sanitary behavior be passed on from generation to generation by symbolic communication, much as we might pass on behavior in our society? To answer that question Rothenbuhler crossed young queens and drones of sanitary and unsanitary strains and discovered that the unsanitary trait was genetically dominant—none of the offspring behaved in sanitary fashion. When he crossed the hybrid offspring with one another he found that *their* offspring fell into four categories: (1) completely unsanitary, (2) completely sanitary, (3) able to uncap cells, and (4) able to remove dead larvae, exactly what one would have expected had the trait been controlled by two independent sets of genes.

Notice the lack of "intelligence" in what at first glance appears to be extremely intelligent behavior. Among the bees that could only uncap the cells, the dead larvae would be left to rot in the opened cells; no move would be made to remove the corpses. Such conduct would be inexcusable in a human janitor, but the bees had no choice. They were unable to perform the rest of the task, and could not learn how.

Are bees then unable to learn anything? Hardly! A bee must be able to learn quickly which flowers are yielding nectar on any day that it flies out to forage. This involves speedy learning of color and odor distinctions, and sometimes of more abstract information communicated by means of a "dance" performed by other foraging bees. To take an example, if a bee is presented with a particular flower odor at the same time it is given sugar water, the flower odor alone will cause it to prepare to feed after *one* presentation of the two stimuli together. We know of no instance of such positive conditioning that can be established so quickly in any primate, including human beings. However, although bees can learn certain narrow classes of behavioral patterns extremely well, they do not have a *general* ability to learn. Instead, they have a limited number of individual, specialized learning abilities. Why is this?

If you closely examine a bee you will notice that its head is not much bigger than the head of a pin, with a brain that is even smaller. The number of cells in its brain is probably comparable to the number of transistors in the "brain" of a sophisticated space probe. A nerve cell is far more versatile in its responses than any transistor, so the preceding comparison is not as apt as it may at first appear. Nevertheless, consider the kinds of behavior of which a space probe is capable. Only a limited number of actions are available to it, and each of those is called up by a very specific stimulus—some change in the surrounding conditions or a command from earth.

In the same way, the small size of the insect brain limits the potential range of its behavior. Learning apparently requires the operation of nerve circuits containing many neurons. If the relationships of the neurons are laid down according to a predetermined genetic program, far fewer nerve circuits are required. A designer operating under these constraints would probably devote as little as possible of the limited neural resources available to him to learning, for he could get a lot more behavior from this tiny organic computer if the capability for that behavior were "hardwired" to begin with. The price to be paid for that would be its flexibility. The insect brain is limited in its ability to confront novel situations. But who can criticize the results? Insects do very well for themselves indeed.

CULTURALLY TRANSMITTED BEHAVIOR

It seems reasonable to suppose that the vast majority of behavioral adaptations that make honeybee society possible are genetically inherited. Put differently, bee society is based on genetically transmitted information. But is this true of all societies?

It is almost universally true of the more complex ones. There are only a few groups of organisms that construct elaborate societies with the kinds of division of labor and sophisticated social interaction one sees in a beehive, and most of them are insects—wasps, bees, ants, and termites. To the extent that these have been investigated, it appears that their societies have much the same basis as that of the honeybee. There is, however, one elaborate society as yet unmentioned.

Unless one considers simple organisms such as sponges to be cellular societies, the only society outside of the insects with substantial division of labor and role differentiation is human society. Indeed, the complexity of our society far overshadows that of any insect, and rests on a far different informational base.

In many developing countries one may readily meet individuals whose grandparents hunted food with spears and arrows, but who themselves use high-powered rifles and hunt only as a hobby. Their vocations may be those of any nation that has been technologically sophisticated for generations: physician, lawyer, or engineer. What is more, if they are transplanted to a developed nation they can fit into the society on equal terms with those whose ancestors have lived under increasingly more technological conditions since the Industrial Revolution. Obviously, people of almost any societal background can learn roles that fit them for a place in almost any other society. In many cases they may not actually do so, but the ability is there. How do people learn their social roles?

There is more than one answer to that, but the most important means seems to be by language. Through language one can learn the most abstract concepts the mind can frame. There is even evidence that the mind is best able to frame that which can be described by language. So it is very important to understand what we mean by language. In a very broad sense, almost all signaling behavior can be considered language, whether conscious or not. Thus one can speak of body language, the language of love, the language of the bees, and more, without meaning anything comparable to language in the strict sense. What are the distinctive characteristics of human language that set it off from all other means of communication?

First, *human language is symbolic.* It employs a code system whose units stand for certain objects or concepts, so that it is possible to deal with those things even when they are not present. A teacher need not bring a cow into the classroom to discuss cattle husbandry. This factor distinguishes language from such behaviors as alarm calls among certain birds or mammals. Some animals may be able to learn that a predator is dangerous without actually being injured, but the learner must see the predator and have an opportunity to associate it with the alarm call produced by those more knowledgeable than itself.

Second, *the symbols themselves are learned*, along with their meanings. This allows language to be almost infinitely flexible, because new symbols can be invented for each new fact or concept. As knowledge grows, vocabulary develops both in comprehensiveness and in subtlety. This trait distinguishes it from "language" such as that of bees, which, although able to convey information about things not close at hand, employs symbols whose meaning is instinctively understood by other bees. A sanitary bee cannot communicate the need of corpse removal to an unsanitary bee. The necessary symbols do not exist in bee language, and they cannot be invented.

Third, *the symbols are related to one another by a syntax.* A child might see a duck swimming in the water and call it a "water bird." Obviously, *water* is used here as an adjective modifying the noun *bird*. It refines the symbolic image of the bird, and is only secondarily a symbol in its own right. A trained chimpanzee, however, might also express "water bird" in sign language. The question is, What does the ape mean by this? It may simply be coincidentally expressing two nouns—*water* (which it sees), and *bird* (which it also sees). In some human languages, syntax is expressed by word order, in others by word endings and prefixes, and in still others by intonations. Whatever form it takes, all human language employs a definite syntax that explicitly indicates the interrelationships of the symbols used.

We may then define language as a symbolic form of communication employing syntax in which the meanings of the symbols must be learned. Note that this is not an arbitrary definition; it is simply a description—one that makes clear the uniqueness of human language. It may well be the most significant human adaptation, because almost all of human culture is dependent on it.

Can human language be considered an adaptation in the same sense as an opposable thumb? Neurological research has identified several portions of the cerebral cortex that are specialized for the production, reception, and interpretation of language. If any of these is damaged, results vary from complete inability to speak to various speech and comprehension disorders. These brain areas are far less well-developed in other mammals, including other primates.

Furthermore, much laborious effort is required to teach whatever "language" apes are able to master, and then they cannot learn more than a few words of human speech, such as "cup" or "mama." Better results have been achieved with sign language and synthetic computer-assisted languages that involve pushing buttons and the like. Nevertheless, in spite of battalions of researchers and often hundreds of pounds of electronic equipment, the vocabulary of even the most well-trained apes remains far below that of many human idiots.

The most important distinctive of human language acquisition, however, is that it does not require instrumental conditioning as a technique of instruction (as in the case of apes). The normal development of speech in a human infant requires no formal instruction at all. Instead, the child learns inductively, first constructing broad syntactic principles, then gradually refining his understanding of grammar as he broadens his vocabulary. Almost all of this learning is based on interaction with others, such as his parents. It is not a passive process of observation—children of deaf mutes cannot learn to speak just by watching television. Language learning is a profoundly social, interpersonal activity in which adult and child continuously modify one another's behavior. If instrumental conditioning is involved at all, it is minimal. No child is born knowing a language, but every normal child is born knowing how to learn one. Human language is a learned behavior, but the ability to learn it is innate, placed in the human genome by the hand of the Creator.

HUMAN UNIQUENESS

In spite of the vast differences between so much of human and animal behavior and the far greater complexity of certain forms of human behavior, the evolutionist asserts that human behavior has continuity with that of other animals, and has in fact developed from that of animal ancestors. Such phenomena as dominance hierarchies, territoriality, interpersonal distance zones, and pair bonding are said to have their equivalents in human society, equivalents that have often been inherited without substantial change from subhuman origins. Even such highly metamorphosed traits as religion and altruism are supposedly traceable to the same roots. The creationist simply asserts that at least the positive aspects of human behavior were created along with the rest of the human organism. Can the evolutionist prove his point?

In order to prove that human evolution is responsible for particular behavioral adaptations, it would be necessary to establish (1) that those behaviors are genetically determined in both human and subhuman, (2) that they are adaptive in both human and subhuman, and above all, (3) that they are homologous. Failure to establish any of those would nullify the proposed evolutionary relationship.

GENETICALLY DETERMINED HUMAN BEHAVIOR

Thirty years ago one could hardly find a professor in the social sciences who would admit that *any* human behavior was genetically determined. If there were human "instincts" they were considered to be limited to the most elemental activities—elimination of waste and breathing. All other behavior (it was asserted) was learned, and most of it culturally transmitted.

All of that was said, however, essentially with only negative evidence—if one can even call it that. Because almost all behavior is absent from the human infant, almost none of it can be innate, was the reasoning. This is, of course, a naive non sequitur. (The same could be said of a larval bee.) What should have been said is that it is very hard to know which behavior is learned and which is innate, because human beings do not develop normally except in contact with other human beings.

Even thus qualified, such a statement is significant. If it is so hard to demonstrate, then inflexible and innate behavior must be at best a very minor component of the total human behavioral repertoire. It is obvious, however, that our genes do set limits on what behavior is possible for us, and that may introduce a kind of bias into our development that could predispose us to certain kinds of conduct. This is often said to explain the existence of so-called cultural universals. Anthropology texts will explain, for instance, that all known human societies contain some version of the incest taboo. The specifics of what is considered incest are culturally determined and vary widely, but (so runs the argument) that shows that even genetically biased behavior is greatly influenced by culture. When the argument descends to this level, one may justly label it an unfalsifiable hypothesis that casts very little light on the problem of human origins. For the creationist, the degree to which human behavior is genetically determined is of little importance (with certain exceptions such as original sin), except to the extent that it may relate to the question of whether or not human nature has undergone substantial evolution.

THE ADAPTIVENESS OF ALTRUISM

One of the great stumbling blocks for evolutionary theory has been the adaptive value of altruism, not only in human beings but in other organisms that display it. One can fairly easily demonstrate the adaptive value of territoriality or dominance hierarchies.[1] Anything that minimizes conflict is valuable to all concerned, for even the winner of a fight may be injured in it. But how can we account for the evolution of a barbed stinger in a worker bee? When she uses it she loses it, along with half her viscera. But bees continue to fight suicidally almost to the last warrior in defense of their society. The worker bee is more than expendable—she is disposable! How can this be explained?

It is significant that the barbs are restricted to *worker* bees. The queen, who is the only female in the hive who can reproduce, has a smooth stinger that can be used any number of times without harm to the user. To an extent, her smooth stinger is compensated for by a larger venom supply, but it is still true that a smooth stinger is less effective than a barbed one. Even after it is severed from a honeybee's body, the barbed stinger and its associated viscera continue to pump venom into the victim's body, resulting in a larger dose than the queen could possibly deliver. But it is obvious that this works to the worker bee's disadvantage. So who benefits?

Recall that the Darwinian precept of "survival of the fittest" does not apply primarily to the fittest *individual*. Whatever promotes the reproduction of a particular gene will tend to increase its frequency in a population. The survival and prosperity of the individual in whom the gene resides will ordinarily tend to promote the reproduction of that gene, unless the individual is sterile. Thus the worker bees are genetically nonexistent, except by proxy.

---

1. A full discussion of these concepts is beyond the scope of this book, but territoriality is the tendency to defend a particular part of an organism's range. Male songbirds, for example, fight any rivals that come too close to their territory, and they sing to warn the intruders away. Dominance hierarchies are also known as "peck orders" such as those that define social rank in a flock of chickens. Behaviors analogous to these are easily observed, of course, in human beings. But are they homologous?

At first glance it would appear to be impossible for an individual to pass on genes to the next generation vicariously, but that is not the case. Indeed, it is not too far from what social insects actually do. Although the worker bees do not share *all* their mother's genes, each of them shares half the genes, and in a large hive they may well have *all* the queen bee's genes among them. Genetically, then, the workers can be viewed as extensions of the queen bee. By their labors they pass on their own genes by proxy even though each is individually sterile. What they so sacrificially defend is not really the hive. It is the *queen*.

Such behavior even occurs in vertebrates to some degree, although in simpler vertebrate societies it is much less marked, as in the case of the acorn woodpecker of western North America, or the Florida jay. These birds form social groups, all of whose members are related to one another, but only a few of whose members reproduce at any one time. Similar arrangements have been described in fish and mammals. Arguing a posteriori, evolutionists contend that such arrangements must sometimes be more advantageous than uncooperative reproduction, since after all they *do* exist.

This kind of thinking can be extended to account for the development of altruistic behavior among all social animals, including human beings, as was accomplished in 1975 by the publication of a significant book, *Sociobiology.* Its author was the entomologist Edward O. Wilson of Harvard University. Initially this book collected very laudatory reviews from members of the biological establishment, but that happy situation did not long prevail, for sociobiology soon attracted the attention of a Marxist group that called itself "Science for the People." Members of the group engaged Wilson and his followers in vigorous and strident debate in every forum to which they could gain access.

Many members of "Science for the People" are competent biologists well able to deal with the arguments of sociobiology. Their motivation can be appreciated when one remembers that one of the basic tenets of Marxism is the perfectibility of man. For Karl Marx, all social evils are produced by our economic systems, especially (but not exclusively) capitalism. Socialism can be expected to replace capitalism by revolution, but even when established, socialism will take time to remedy the evils of capitalism. In fact, socialism itself can be expected to produce a degree of evil because of lingering capitalistic influences within socialism. Ultimately, socialists believe the state will wither away (there being no further need for its existence), and we will all live together in peace, harmony, and social perfection.

One of the reasons Marxism is incompatible with Christianity is that the Scriptures insist that mankind is *not* perfectible, that we suffer from an evil nature implanted by the fall of Adam. In fact, it is the peccability of human nature that established the need for grace, substitutionary atonement, and salvation, all of which are vigorously rejected by Marxism. Suddenly sociobiology entered the picture with its own version of original sin—a version that saw it as a remnant of man's essential animal nature, not as a remnant of his creation and subsequent fall. If we are constrained by our genes to be territorial and thus wage war, to form dominance hierarchies and thus establish tyranny, we are not as perfectible as Marx thought us to be. But unlike Christianity, sociobiology offers no salvation.

BEHAVIORAL HOMOLOGY

Two points were established earlier in this book that are essential to what follows. They are (1) that the scientific method works best in real time; it is exceedingly difficult to establish historical events or their meaning by the scientific method, because retrodicted facts are usually open to a variety of interpretations, and (2) that it is very difficult even for an evolutionist to decide whether two similar adaptations are merely analogous or homologous. Given these uncertainties, the following points can be made:

1. When dealing with an organism of such broad behavioral capacity as a human being, it is virtually impossible to know whether a trait such as territoriality or dominance is learned or inherited.
2. Even when a behavioral trait appears to have a genetic basis, there is no obvious way to know if it has the *same* genetic basis as that exhibited by some other organism. We cannot know, therefore, if it has been inherited by both from a common ancestor.
3. Behavior does not fossilize. It can only be inferred from fossil evidence. Thus numerous dinosaur footprints occurring together may indicate herd behavior in those animals, a true social interaction. But it could indicate equally well that they were all attracted to a favorable set of environmental conditions, much as flies may congregate in a warm place in autumn. There is no unambiguous fossil evidence whatever that can tell us about the behavior of our alleged early primate forbears.
4. We are most likely to see ourselves in any animal mirror we

hold up. In past centuries animals were thought to possess a moral nature similar to human beings, and when "guilty" of some offense (murder, for instance) were sometimes dressed in human clothes and executed by hanging or burning at the stake. Today we see biologists and social scientists speaking of barter, role playing, culture, ritual, magic, and tribalism among animals. These are human behaviors, and designating superficially similar traits by labels derived from human society creates bias in our studies.

Imagine for a moment that an experimenter has attached a piece of food to a strong stake by a heavy cotton string. An ape encountering the food would not be able to obtain it easily. After considerable investigation the ape would discover the string attached to the food, chew through it, and get the food. Most investigators would be impressed with that as an example of "insight," the highest form of cognitive behavior, supposed to be at its best in human beings. Surely this experiment seems highly persuasive evidence for behavior continuity between us and the apes, with whom we supposedly share a common ancestry. However, the behavior we have just described was actually observed not in an ape, but in a dung beetle!

Much human culture may not be adaptive in a genetic sense; that is, we may have culturally propagated behavioral traits that do not correspond to genes and neither promote nor hinder their transmission, but which may play a role in the function of the culture itself. Sociobiology explains *too* much—a characteristic it shares with the rest of evolutionary thought. A thorough literature search can uncover an attempted explanation of practically any human or animal behavior in terms of natural selection. But if any conceivable behavior could be explained in such terms, there is still no plausible way to falsify the hypothesis that says natural selection has produced *any* (and every) kind of behavior. This consideration alone is almost enough to place sociobiology, at least for the time being, in the category of pseudoscience.

The most cogent objection has been saved for last: *all* society has an informational basis. We have seen that in social insects the overwhelming majority of this societal information is encoded in the DNA of their cellular nuclei. As even Edward Wilson avers, though such traits as territoriality and dominance may be innate in us the vast majority of the information necessary for human social behavior is culturally transmitted, mainly by language. In culture, the informational equivalent of a gene would be ideational—a concept or idea, for instance. Population genetics posits that favorable genes tend to spread in time throughout the total gene pool of a species, but that obviously would be a slow process, and its frequency and importance is doubtful. Such a spread of favorable genes would be trivial compared to the effects of ideas or the speed with which they spread through society, producing cultural change. Bee society might change over the course of millennia by genetic mechanisms; human society changes rapidly enough to bewilder us all. The most important determinant of human behavior is the behavior of other humans. Therefore, the propagation of one's ideas and attitudes is potentially far more influential than the propagation of one's genes.

The Christian may well hope that in the long run the concepts of sociobiology will not be widely accepted. Sociobiology's potential as an argument for human evolution is actually not its greatest threat. In a more recent book, *On Human Nature,* Wilson suggests that all of our present religious and political ideologies will be replaced in the future by what he calls "the evolutionary epic," which he considers "the best myth we will ever have."

By this Wilson does not mean that evolution is false. He is using the word *myth* in a special sense, as a rationalization for a system of belief and its existential basis. In other words, what Wilson proposes as a substitute for religion, or even as a religion in its own right, is evolution.

Every religion has an apologetic structure, part of whose task is to dispatch rival ideologies. In an interview appearing in the May 1982 issue of *Science Digest,* reporter Jeffrey Saver states that Wilson "hopes that sociobiology's ability to present a fully satisfactory, evolutionary account of religion itself will constitute the deathblow science gives to many of the traditional assumptions of theology" (p. 86).

How might he hope to accomplish this? As we shall see in the next chapter, religion is unique to human beings. But many other organisms exhibit behaviors that may be considered unique. The dance of the bees is unique; the courtship rituals of the bowerbirds are unique. If religion is not the consequence of mankind's creation in the image of God, but has evolved simply as an adaptation to the human life-style, then its explanation is no more supernatural than that of any other trait, human or animal. And now that sociobiology knows it for an evolutionary vestige, perhaps it should be got rid of, even as we pull out those other, potentially troublesome evolutionary vestiges—our wisdom teeth! It is imperative that Christian scholarship lose no time in interesting itself in sociobiology and taking its implications very seriously.

8

THE STUDY OF MANKIND

According to Scripture, man was made in the image of God, something that is said of no other creature. However, exactly what is meant by being made in the image of God has always been a puzzle. A physical resemblance surely is not intended, for Scripture also teaches that God's essential nature is nonmaterial (John 4:24). Furthermore, despite their many undeniable similarities to us, it seems clear that a radical discontinuity exists between animals and ourselves.

THE STUDY OF MAN

Anthropology, the study of human beings, can be approached from one of two major directions. *Cultural anthropology* deals with man's patterns of living, especially his social life. *Physical anthropology* deals specifically with man's physical body and its past history. The anthropological studies most relevant for our purposes are those that deal with similarities and differences between man and certain other creatures.

There are several ways in which human beings are anatomically unique, but the same could be said of panda bears. It must be more than that. Two possibilities suggest themselves: Is man intellectually unique? Is he spiritually unique? It would seem that mankind does indeed stand almost alone in the intellectual sphere, and that he is totally without company in the spiritual.

Human beings have developed various patterns of culture largely because they are not bound by instinct, are flexible, and have great ability to think, learn, use symbols, and speak. Among the structurally simple animals, instinctive behavior seems to predominate, as we discussed in Chapter 7. Even communication and other social behaviors possessed by animals cannot be divorced from their involuntary and instinctive reactions. It is true that human behavior is to some degree instinctive, but no one could argue intelligently that because of this humans are the same as animals. That would be to ignore the vast differences between humans and the rest of creation and to emphasize small similarities way out of reasonable proportion. The many differences of degree that *do* separate the behavior of man and animal are so great that they amount to differences of "kind."

It does not take a master's degree in biology to distinguish a human being from an ape; a short catalog of the more significant differences might include human bipedalism, absent from the apes who walk on their knuckles in a semiquadruped fashion, or swing Tarzan-like through the trees. Bipedalism requires the distinctively human spinal curvature, pelvic shape, relative length of the legs, large gluteus maximus, and anterior placement of the foramen magnum of the skull (which permits us to look in a forward direction when standing upright without straining our necks). Our gift of speech is reflected in specialized brain areas, and our completely opposable thumbs permit us to manipulate objects far more delicately than can the cleverest chimpanzee. These differences, however, are trivial *within* the far greater anatomical similarities that we and the apes share. They are important human adaptations that fit us for our special way of life, but it is that life-style itself that is truly unique.

Among the most distinctive of human traits is the ability to make and use tools. The Galapagos woodpecker finch uses cactus spines as tools to dig insects out of crevices, and an African species of hawk smashes eggs with rocks to eat them. Sea otters do the same to sea urchins, and some degree of tool use can be observed among wild chimpanzees. But that is all vastly different from human tool use.

Every human culture has its distinctive tool kit, and those of even the simplest human cultures far outweigh those employed by animals. We teach our children how to use these tools, and we teach them how to make them as well. No child is born knowing how to use a screwdriver. Apes may teach their young to make some simple tools and shelters (although all the evidence is not in yet). One thing is certain, though: they do not *tell* their young how to make them. It is the cultural transmission of technology that makes the breadth and sophistication of the human tool kit possible. Like other manifestations of symbolic language, that cultural transmission of technology is totally absent among the animals. Whether such has *always* been the case is, of course, another matter. For all we know, some presently extinct animals

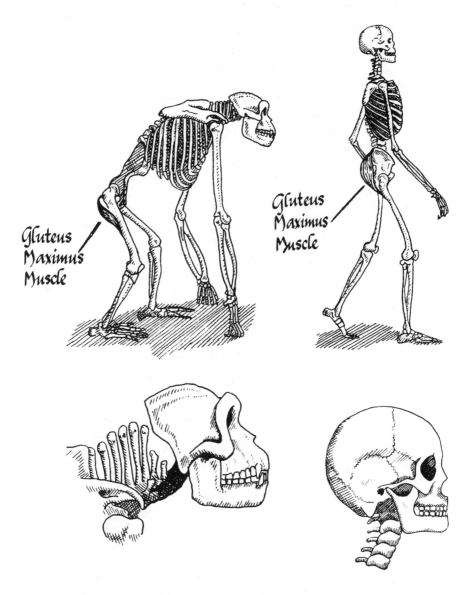

Figure 8.1 Some differences in adaptations of human beings and a representative great ape, the gorilla. The human's upright stance requires a doubly curved spinal column and a large gluteus maximus muscle. The junction of the spinal vertebrae and skull is farther forward in the human, permitting the head to balance efficiently when the body is upright. Note also the more massive gorilla jaw and the heavy bony crest at the top of the skull, needed for anchorage of the muscles moving the jaw.

may have had far greater toolmaking ability than do any that survive today, and some of the simple fossil tools found by archaeologists and anthropologists may not have been made by human beings at all. It is not out of the question that such clearly nonhuman creatures as *Australopithecus* may have made tools as instinctively as a spider spins a web.

But the religious dimension of humanity is even more distinctive than the technological. Religious ideas are found in all known cultures past and present, and there is good evidence for their presence even among Neanderthal people. *Homo sapiens* means "thinking man," but *Homo religiosum* might be a better designation. We are religious far more consistently than we are rational, and in view of the biblical account of creation that ought not to be surprising. "Thou has made us for Thyself," Augustine mused, "and our hearts are restless till they find their rest in Thee." It is this trait, totally without precedent among other animals, that marks us out most surely as more than animals, sociobiology notwithstanding.

HUMAN EVOLUTIONARY THEORY

Most contemporary anthropologists believe that mankind evolved from tree-dwelling ancestors who descended to the ground and became terrestrial. Such an ancestor would have resembled a simian much more than a human being of today, but would not have been exactly the same as a modern great ape. Two basic choices would have been open to this protohominid, as some call him. He could have become a browsing, forest-dwelling animal like the modern gorilla. That would have required a heavy body and great strength to force his way through undergrowth, and like the gorilla he probably never would have fully adopted the biped stance. With the forefeet needed for locomotion, they would not have been free for tool use. Thus the intellectual stimulation that accompanies the development of a technological culture would not have been open to him, and high intelligence would have had no more value for him than for any other beast (some of which, like rats, do very well without it). Natural selection would not have helped to develop it.

The alternative would have been to become an inhabitant of parkland or veld, where low vegetation and ground cover are at a minimum. This is the choice that many evolutionary anthropologists believe the protohominid actually took. Studies of baboons and "lower" monkeys that pursue such a life today tend to show that the use of a simple digging stick would have more than doubled the food supply of those animals. That baboons do not ordinarily eat meat is probably (at least partly) because of their lack of a cultural tradition favoring it. Most monkeys and apes can be trained to eat and enjoy meat (some meat *is* eaten under natural conditions), although their diet is mainly vegetarian. If baboons had some means of capturing and killing other animals (particularly large game), their food supply would be increased greatly.

It is obvious that baboons that would have developed a tradition of tool use for food-gathering and hunting would have had a great advantage over those that did not. They also would have so successfully competed with their less endowed colleagues that after a number of generations only tool-using baboons would have existed. This would be true even if the tool users were not especially more intelligent than the nonusers. The bipedalism necessary for effective use of tools would have developed at the beginning of this process as a means of increasing speed afoot, which is necessry for life in the African savannah.

Once a tradition of effective tool use was developed, natural selection would tend to favor those that could use the tools most efficiently—that is, most intelligently. In this way, culture would favor the development of intelligence, and intelligence would permit the development of a more sophisticated culture. The use of tools would also favor bipedalism, for as we have mentioned, the hands must be free for effective tool use. If a faculty of communication such as speech could be developed in conjunction with tool use, the whole process of cultural advancement would be facilitated greatly; and the earth, we presume, would be inherited by advanced baboons.

Perhaps that scenario, for which there is no evidence whatever, is unappealing. If so, it is not the only one that has been proposed. Consider this alternative: the original protohominid spent more time on the ground than the modern chimpanzee does, but like the chimpanzee it was a forest dweller. However, chimpanzees are not truly bipedal. As an adaptation to a semiterrestrial or terrestrial existence, both the chimpanzee and the gorilla use knuckle-walking as a form of locomotion (they clench their fists somewhat and use their knuckles and arms to support their forequarters). That is why they cannot be called fully bipedal, although they can temporarily adopt a bipedal posture, especially when running. The protohominid never developed this knuckle-walking posture because it quickly acquired the habit of carrying things in its arms.

Our first reconstruction of hominid evolution argued that tool use, carrying, and the like were made possible by bipedalism. Bipedalism, according to this view, evolved as a rapid form of locomotion appropriate to running about on the ground in the savannah. The revisionist reconstruction criticizes this view, pointing out that in its earliest stages bipedalism would have been ambiguous as an adaptation to fast running, because early bipedalism would not have been fast. Put more simply, a semiquadrupedal quasibiped could hardly have walked, let alone run. It would have needed to get up into the trees to escape its enemies, trees that would not have been there on the savannah. But trees *would* have been present in the forest habitat that the revisionists propose.

But if bipedalism did not arise as an adaptation for speedy running, what purpose could it have served? Perhaps it was initially a reproductive adaptation, it is now argued. If the nuclear family (parents and a single generation of children) was an early hominid behavioral trait, the father would have had an advantage over other males who could not contribute to the feeding of the young. In other animals that bring food to their young a variety of adaptations are used to carry it. In carnivores and many birds food is brought home to the young in the crop or stomach and regurgitated for feeding. If the protohominid male brought food back to his mate and children he would have had to carry it in his hands. The hands would therefore have become unavailable to assist in locomotion. The adaptive advantage of bipedalism would have tended to force itself on those creatures even before they became toolmakers. Ultimately they could put their liberated hands to use making tools and weapons.

We want to emphasize that the foregoing hypothetical story of baboons and other stories like it that depict prehuman history are speculative and lack hard supporting evidence. There are no bones, arrowheads, or any other finds that compel belief in such a story. The kind of evidence we *do* possess is twofold: (1) fossils of various extinct primates and certain forms of man, and (2) remnants of the cultures of some of those in the form of chipped stone implements and the like. From this evidence we may draw a few conclusions about early man.

The following is a summary of some of the major types of fossils thought to bear close relationship to modern man. This is not intended to support in any way the teaching that man evolved from subhuman ancestors. Careful reading will show that we intend to demonstrate the humanity of certain fossil forms, and where this is not possible (as in Australopithecines from Africa), we shall show the absence of a connection with the human race. Since the terminology employed for these fossils is in a constant state of flux, we have usually given several names for each fossil.

1. Australopithecines (including *Australopithecus* [*Zinjanthropus*], and *Homo habilis/modjokertensis*, "Lucy"). These

are regarded as the most primitive of the hominids, or manlike primates. There seem to be many varieties, and a lively controversy is proceeding as to their proper names and the relationships they bear to one another. There are "robust" and "gracile" forms, for instance, with most evolutionary anthropologists associating the gracile types more intimately with a phylogenetic line leading to modern man.

Although it is becoming a minority view, it was once widely held that Australopithecines possessed a material culture, as indicated by pebble tools. But the presence of artifacts associated with their bones is open to alternative explanations and interpretations. One is that the cultural artifacts are the products of Pithecanthropines (see below) that may have hunted and eaten *Australopithecus*.

According to a computerized multivariate analysis of the measurements and proportions of the pelvis of modern apes, man, and a gracile Australopithecine (Sterkfontein), the *Australopithecus* pelvis was different from rather than intermediate between those of man and ape. In our opinion, no compelling evidence has yet been presented that *Australopithecus* was a cultural animal, or that it was ancestral to man. Even if some were bipedal (possibly "Lucy") and somewhat cultural, these traits would not be sufficient to make them human or even near-human.

2. *Homo erectus* (Pithecanthropines). These are creatures of approximately human stature and posture that have been found in Asia (Java man, Peking man), Africa, and Europe (Heidelberg man?). It is almost beyond dispute that these creatures had material cultures consisting of hand axes, perhaps spears or digging sticks, and fire. Their cranial capacity was generally smaller than that of modern humans, although some specimens approach or meet the lower limit of the modern human brain volume. In our opinion it is possible that these creatures were human, although there is no clearcut evidence of any religious life among them. It is possible that some were specialized or degenerate branches of humanity.

3. Neanderthaloids *(Homo sapiens)*. It has been shown that these people stood as erect as we do. Their cranial capacity was as great and often greater than that of modern man, but their forehead was lower. Their skeletal structure was very heavy, and it differed from ours more than those of living races differ from one another. They must have been extremely muscular, powerful people. Nevertheless, if one

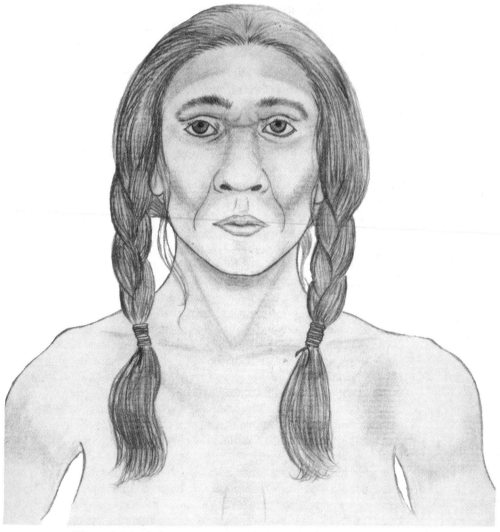

Figure 8.2 Artist's reconstruction of a Neanderthal woman. All modern primitive peoples dress the hair. It is likely that Neanderthal people did so also.

could meet the average Neanderthaloid in a crowd he would not seem to fall outside the normal range of human variation, and one would probably pass him without astonishment.

The Neanderthaloids were responsible for the so-called Mousterian chipped stone culture—a culture that was shared by some Cro-Magnoids who were indisputably human. It has been suggested that the Neanderthaloids were a specialized race of people who perhaps were isolated by glacial action. Perhaps their physical characteristics were influenced by inbreeding, selection for a cold environment of northern forests, and an especially vigorous life-style based on close-encounter hunting and killing of big game. Thus it would have been desirable for them to be able to climb over fallen tree trunks with greater agility than we could employ and to hang onto big game while dispatching it. Grave sites of Neanderthaloids have been found that are very similar to those of modern "primitives," and such sites seem to indicate a religious life in the Neanderthaloids comparable to that which accompanies burials in some modern nonliterate cultures.

It is our opinion that Neanderthal man was entirely human, although racially distinct. It is even probable that people of European and Middle Eastern descent may count him among their ancestors. It is of interest that the least human-appearing Neanderthaloids were not the earliest of them but the latest, and that (in early postglacial times) when contact between Neanderthals and other *Homo sapiens* became possible, several populations (for example, at Mr. Carmel in Israel) seem to show evidence of hybridization between the two. The evidence is more than suggestive, therefore, that Neanderthal man is a member in very good standing of the human race.

4. Cro-Magnon man *(Homo sapiens)*. This was a human being in every respect and doubtless was our ancestor—an ancestor of whom we can be proud in many ways. His artistic sense (within the framework of the media available to him) is unexcelled to the present day. There is ample evidence both of high intelligence and a sensitive spiritual nature in him. His religion apparently involved fetishes, sympathetic magic (judging from his cave paintings), and still other practices that exist even today among culturally primitive societies. In many ways the culture of some Cro-Magnon peoples equals that of the modern Eskimo. Unfortunately, there is ample indication of the darker side of human character among them.

Cro-Magnon man seems to have fought and killed those of his own kind and Neanderthals as well.

Evolutionists have been unable to demonstrate that any of those forms have been ancestral (in the evolutionary sense) to modern man or to other varieties of hominids (with the exception of Cro-Magnon and Neanderthal, who were obviously human). There is even good evidence that forms of *Australopithecus* and *Homo erectus* (possibly *Homo sapiens* as well) existed contemporaneously. Therefore, we cannot see how the fossil evidence can be in conflict with the opening chapters of Genesis. Australopithecines were almost certainly not human beings, and the other forms probably were various specialized offshoots of the main trunk of human ancestry, some likely being degenerate forms. A more objective understanding of possible relationships (or the lack thereof) among the many fossils probably would be facilitated if evolutionists could be relieved of their obsession to fit all data into an evolutionary scheme regardless of the difficulties.

We believe that our first ancestors were human in every way and were created in precisely the manner described in the book of Genesis. The variety of human races and types today attests to changes that have taken place in humanity since that day (apparently rather rapidly), but these are very small changes indeed. The changes from man's earliest fossil races to modern racial types seem to be an example of diversification. The evidence does not indicate a transitional series beginning with the lower primates and leading to human beings.

"What is the question," asked Benjamin Disraeli, "now placed before society with the glib assurance which to me is most astonishing? That question is this: Is man an ape or an angel? I, my lords, I am on the side of the angels."

Yet that is not quite what Scripture has to teach about the nature of man. "Thou hast made him a little lower than [the angels]," wrote David in Psalm 8:5, "and dost crown him with glory and majesty." Neither ape nor angel, man has the honor of bearing a familial resemblance to the very Master of the universe, for it was God Himself who fashioned him and breathed into his nostrils the breath of life.

9

THE BIBLE AND CREATION

Many religious writers (and even some scientific writers such as Kerkut) have criticized the doctrine of evolution without offering alternatives. Such criticism does serve a valuable purpose, but it is the responsibility of the Christian not just to criticize, but to criticize *constructively*, and where possible to propose alternative views with fewer shortcomings than those of evolutionary theory. Such a theory, to be adequate, must take full account of all scientific data. And if it is to be Christian, it must additionally accept and build upon biblical revelation as valid information.

THE AUTHORITY OF THE BIBLE

For the Christian, including the scientist who is a Christian, there is no higher authority than the Bible, the inspired Word of God. This is the means by which God has chosen to communicate with man. It is not our purpose here to discuss the various detailed theories that attempt to harmonize the biblical creation narrative with scientific discoveries.[1] The first two chapters of Genesis contain the primary biblical information on creation. This portion of the Bible has been the object of numerous books and articles by many scholars. At the present time not all Christians agree on the interpretation of all that is written in Genesis 1-2, but in spite of that, certain truths stand out.

First, God is the Creator. His power and will are manifested in bringing the earth and all living things into existence.

Second, there is order in the creative activities. There is a division of six days, the seventh being the original Sabbath, on which no work was done. On the third day plant life was created; on

---

1. For a summary, see Davis Young, "Genesis: Neither More Nor Less," *Eternity*, May 1982, pp. 14-21; or W. H. Johns, "Strategies for Origins," *Ministry*, 54(5), —1981, pp. 26-28.

the fifth, birds and sea creatures; and on the sixth, various kinds of animals, and finally man himself.

Third, man was clearly the climax of creation. Man was last in order, but first in importance. As a living being (soul), he shared the breath of life with other created things; but stamped with the image of God, he possessed a spiritual nature that made him unique among all forms of life.[2]

Fourth, (and most controversial, even among creationists), the entire process of biological creation appears to have been completed in a very short period of time.

There has been considerable debate among Christians regarding the length of the days referred to in the creation account. Some evangelical scholars have interpreted the days of creation in such a way as to bring them into accord with current concepts of geology. The temptation to do so is understandable (and thus to avoid a few of the major conflicts between science and the Bible), but such attempts usually involve imposing an a priori structure upon the interpretation of Scripture. Most words in any language have a somewhat flexible range of meanings, and in the final analysis their meaning is determined not by a lexicon but by context. As you study Genesis 1 and 2 note how the word for "day" has a similar range of meaning to the English word. One may speak of George Washington's "day" as an indefinite period of time (the context makes this clear), and this is how "day" is used in Genesis 2:4. But if a physician prescribes medicine that is to be taken at one dosage the first day, at a reduced dosage the second day, and so on, something quite definite is meant. We believe that "day" is clearly used in this latter way in Genesis 1:23.

Even setting aside the question of the length of the days of creation, evolution is still not taught in Scripture. Furthermore, although long "days" may *appear* more congenial to evolutionary concepts than twenty-four-hour days, they really substitute new problems for old ones.[3] Although an extensive exegetical discussion of the Genesis days is not possible here, the clearest and simplest rendering of appropriate biblical passages is that the days

---

2. Sin entered the human race after the first man disobeyed God, bringing about the Fall. Sin is not to be thought of as a reversion to any prehuman behavior patterns, but is characteristically human and confined among all organisms to humanity because it involves a violation of moral responsibility that was given only to man.

3. We are left, for example, with plants existing for millennia before there is sun, moon, day or night, a botanical absurdity. Then, if insects and birds are created millennia after plants, pollination would have been impossible and many plants would have died out. Finally, if day six (when Adam was created) was thousands or millions of years long. Adam's age at death would have numbered in the thousands or millions of years, instead of hundreds, as Genesis 5 teaches.

of Genesis were comparable to our own days. We also believe that those days reflect the temporal order of creation events, and of course we agree with Bible scholars who recognize internal harmony among the various biblical passages dealing with creation.[4]

Genesis 1 contains important information regarding the pattern of creation. The word translated "kind" here apparently refers to general reproducing groups of organisms (see Gen. 1:21, 24-25). The term probably does not refer to *species* in most cases, but it may refer to what we today would call genera, families, orders, or other taxonomic categories. The classification now in use is essentially Linnaen and is very helpful. But there is no reason to think that the word *kind* used by Moses about 3,500 years ago is synonymous with our word *species. Species* does not even correspond to *kind* in our language today. Recent studies by Hebrew scholars indicate that the Hebrew word *min* (translated "kind" in the KJV and many other versions of the Bible) may be much broader in its meaning and may correspond to such groupings as family or order in the Linnaen system of taxonomy. It may even have no exact twentieth-century equivalent.

Continued evangelical research may help to define the nature of the Genesis "kind." We can infer that all changes take place only within boundaries set by the creative hand of God, because the Scriptures teach that organisms reproduce "after their kind." Hence no change is capable of causing an organism to move to a kind different from that of its ancestors. For this reason it is important to discover what the boundaries of the kinds are.

There are many biblical reasons for rejecting an evolutionary account of man's origin. For instance, Eve was formed from the body of Adam, and Adam himself was molded by divine transmutation from some type of earth.[5] Descendants of the original man and woman (as well as other creatures) must have been subject to change in a limited sense by diversification, which would account for such things as racial variations in evidence today.

---

4. Because we believe in the inerrancy of Scripture, we are not sympathetic with those who believe that the events of Genesis 2 contradict those of chapter 1. Genesis 1 deals with creation in general, showing man's place in the large pattern. Chapter 2 treats the creation of man in more detail. It is also entirely possible and reasonable to translate certain verbs in Genesis 2 in the pluperfect tense, as does the *New International Version:* "Now the LORD God *had* formed out of the ground all the beasts of the field and all the birds of the air" (Gen. 2:19, italics added). All apparent contradictions disappear when this is done.

5. See H. C. Leupold, *Exposition of Genesis*, pp. 114-16.

"Then the elephant's child sat back on his little haunches and pulled, and pulled, and pulled, and his nose began to stretch. And the crocodile floundered into the water, making it all creamy with great sweeps of his tail, and *he* pulled, and pulled, and pulled." And that, as Rudyard Kipling tells us, is how the elephant got its trunk.

Of course no one believes that story, and probably no one ever really has believed it. In that, it differs from both creation and evolution, each of which is passionately espoused by a multitude of believers. Yet one of them has to be no more than a similar story.

Many who think of themselves as Christian believers are satisfied to leave the biblical creation account in just that category, a charming and instructive fable—but not to be taken seriously as history, and surely not as science. Is that not enough?

It was not enough for the apostle Peter, who, in discussing the reliability and objective validity of Scripture wrote that he had not followed "cleverly devised [fables]" (*mythois*; 2 Pet. 1:16). For Peter, and for the authors of this book, creation is a fact.

According to some, it is evolution that is the fact. In 1982, Dr. Kenneth Saladin and Dr. Charles C. Brooks told members of the American Association for the Advancement of Science, who were assembled for their annual meeting, that they should henceforth call evolution "a fact" and should play down disputes within the scientific community about the manner in which evolution proceeds. Yet, as we hope we have shown, the so-called fact of evolution cannot be proved from the support data used by evolutionists. The theory of evolution is actually neither satisfactory nor entirely plausible, and we believe it often is inspired by an antisupernatural bias. As William B. Provine, writing in the June 1982 issue of *Bioscience* says, "There are no gods and no designing forces. The frequently made assertion that modern biology and the assumptions of the Judeo-Christian tradition are fully compatible is false. Second, there exist no inherent moral or ethical laws, no absolute guiding principles for human society" (p. 506).

Much factual data is inconsistent with the theory in its present form. Arguments for evolution fall into historical and comparative categories. The historical argument treats the geological study of fossils, and the comparative argument treats similarities of anatomy, physiology, biochemistry, embryology, and behavior among organisms. The comparative argument proceeds on the unjustified working assumption that similarities tend to indicate common ancestry.

Christian scholarship has scarcely begun to attack this mountain of scholarly study, but there are strong indications that the evolutionary structure is not sound. The raw data used by evolutionists can be interpreted just as satisfactorily within a creationist framework. Organisms occur in certain natural groupings with minor discontinuities or gaps between those groupings. The Christian need not be burdened with an evolutionary compulsion to explain how such gaps could have been bridged. Some similarities may exist between organisms because of their common ancestry, but most similarities are the result of their creation by one Designer.

EPILOGUE: CREATIONISM'S UNFINISHED BUSINESS

The year was 1960. Seated behind his desk across from me was one of the foremost geneticists and evolutionists of recent times, Dr. Theodosius Dobzhansky, at that time my professor at Columbia University where I was a graduate student. We had been discussing a creationist with whom he had been corresponding for a number of months before breaking off the relationship.

"Oh, you mean the crazy one!" he exclaimed. "You know, he was just as good a scientist as anybody, and was really very knowledgeable."

"But how could he not believe in evolution, if he was all that knowledgeable?" I asked.

"Well," replied Dobzhansky, "he claimed to go by the evidence, but the truth of it is that no conceivable evidence could convince him. I finally decided enough was enough and gave up on him, though at first I respected his convictions."

"Why did you give up?" I asked.

"It was partly because he wanted to publish our correspondence, but also I have come to feel that creationism is blasphemous. Here we are surrounded by the most impressive evidence that evolution has occurred. If it has not occurred, then the creator they make so much of has placed it all here to mislead us. Anybody that can accuse God of a practical joke like that is a blasphemer to my mind."

That gave me plenty to think about. Although I was not at the time a committed creationist, I was moving in that direction. Later, as I walked to the subway I passed St. Paul's Chapel, where I had often spent my lunch hour at the organ concerts regularly given there. I knew that inside was a large stained glass window of Paul preaching to the Athenian scholars. What would Paul have thought of Dr. Dobzhansky's opinions? Perhaps the university

133

motto would serve as a guide: *In lumine tuo videbimus lumen*—
"in Thy light we shall see the light." There was even a Bible
inscription chiseled into the limestone of one of the science
buildings: "Speak to the earth and it shall teach thee." I had looked
up the remainder of the passage once: "And the fishes of the sea
shall declare unto thee. Who knoweth not in all these that the hand
of the LORD hath wrought this?" (Job 12:8-9, KJV).

By 1960 that ignorance of God's work had become widespread
indeed. But was it me who was wrong? Sometimes, set against
overwhelming and nearly universal intellectual opposition, my
belief in either creation or any other Christian teaching seemed as
pointless as believing the earth was flat. Perhaps the truth of it
was that, like Dr. Dobzhansky's correspondent, no evidence would
convince me. What would I believe twenty years from that time?

Anyone who has read this far knows by now what *both* of us as
authors believe. We see the matter as not so much one of evidence
but one of how the evidence is to be interpreted. That, in turn,
depends on a preexisting bias. One of the great myths of history is
that science advances with a pristine, soulless commitment to
truth. But humans are not computers, and if we were neither
science nor any other creative endeavor would be possible for us.
From time to time someone looks at the universe with new eyes
and reassembles the jumble of reality into a fresh pattern.
Conventional discussions of the scientific method have it that the
reality suggests the pattern—to some extent it may. But it is
equally true that the pattern is often decided upon first, and the
facts arranged to fit.

Evolution itself is a classic example from the history of science.
The same kinds of evidence for the theory were widely known in
scientific circles before Darwin's day, but the idea of evolution was
simply not acceptable because no one could propose why it might
take place or what forces could drive it. In fact, when Darwin *did*
propose natural selection as a mechanism, a necessary body of
evidence was actually *missing*—the particulate theory of genetics
that was even then being developed in monastic obscurity by
Mendel. But that lack did not disturb Darwin—he promoted the
hypothesis of pangenes as a substitute!

People did not believe in creation in 1840 because it was credible;
they believed in it because the alternative was incredible. Today
the situation is thoroughly reversed. Creationism will never
become an intellectually acceptable alternative to evolution until it
becomes more convincing than the alternative. To be sure, we
never expect it to replace evolution as the dominant world view (for
reasons that we have already discussed), but we are not far from

the time when creationism may be the inhabitant of an intellectual ghetto if nothing is done to increase its acceptance. It will do no good to demand equal time for creationism in public schools if when we get it the instructors can find nothing positive to say about creationism. Though creation is a fact and is true in the commonly accepted sense, the arguments used by creationists to support it are all too often inadequate or even invalid.

What does creationism need to be convincing?

1. *Creationism needs an uncompromising but civil spirit.* Negativism is to some extent inherent in the very nature of creationism because it is, in effect, the negation of evolution. But we must avoid the intellectual criminalization of our opponents who, despite their bias, are for the most part learned and decent people, honestly convinced that they are right. We must also avoid the temptation to compromise, to fit revelation into an evolutionary mode for the sake of peace. Not only are such compromises unconvincing, but they are a betrayal of the truth. The motivation to persevere in the exceedingly difficult task of reinterpretation and research that faces us will wither if we pretend that there is no real problem after all.

2. *Creationism needs more scholars.* There has been great progress in this area, particularly in the biological sciences, but there is still a pressing need for geologists, astronomers, and others. The most telling arguments for the antiquity of the earth are geological and astronomical in origin. In our opinion they have never been answered satisfactorily by creationists, probably because there are too few committed creationists professionally qualified to deal with the specialized data in these areas. Christian young people need to prayerfully consider entering these fields. We are not qualified to deal with astrophysics; we would like to meet more of those who are, so that some of the questions raised by this discipline can be discussed and answered. Part of the problem is that it is usually extremely difficult for a creationist, however competent and well qualified, to obtain an advanced degree in science at a standard university because of widespread and determined prejudice against creationism in the science faculties of those institutions. It is too early to judge whether or not Christian institutions will be able to fill this need, but it seems likely that financial problems will prevent them from doing so at an academically competent level, even if they are able to find qualified instructors.

3. *Creationism needs more clear-cut biblical foundations.* We

do not believe that the biblical basis of the doctrine of creation has been fully explored despite the years of study that have been devoted to it by Jewish and Christian scholars. It is likely that a great deal of information remains to be mined from the pages of God's Word by those who are spiritually and educationally qualified to do so. This task might best be accomplished by those with a thorough background both in biblical theology and the natural sciences, and who are committed to the verbal plenary inspiration of Scripture. We would like to challenge such students of Scripture to give the study of creation a high priority, to think through its theological implications, and to *publish* the results of their labor.

4. *Creationism needs research.* The sorest points faced by creationists today were also the sorest points of creationism in Darwin's day. Were it not for the almost total ascendency of evolution in scientific thought, creationism today might be a very well-developed discipline. As it is, we creationist scientists too often have retreated into an intellectual shell, leaving the discovery and interpretation of the facts solely to the opposition.

This lack of research is not entirely the fault of creationism, however. Few people realize how very expensive modern biological research has become, or how sophisticated the apparatus must be to allow the researcher to work on the outer borders of scientific knowledge. Almost everything that can be discovered with a scalpel and a light microscope has been discovered. Further advances require instruments costing in the tens or even hundreds of thousands of dollars apiece. The days of the basement researcher are over. Even evolutionists claim to have difficulty here, and have publicly expressed frustration with the estimated thirty million dollars that is spent nationwide on their studies each year. Not even crude estimates are available of the financial support for creation research, but in comparison it can be only the smallest pittance.

But modern research facilities cost the creationist just as much as they do the evolutionist—more, in fact, for the evolutionist generally has at his disposal university and institutional resources unavailable to the average creationist. The evolutionist may also have government or foundation grants available to him, often derived from tax funds, whereas the creationist must usually get along as best he can, on small private donations or on his own funds. Mostly, creationists simply do without, while vital research goes undone.

But if and when this handicap is overcome, creationism will still need clear-cut research goals and some estimate of their priority. Some of those goals we might pick as most in need of attention are the following:

a. *Biogeography.* Even Darwin, to judge from his letters and other personal documents, once believed that the distribution of organisms on the earth could be accounted for by postulating a number of centers of creation from which the inhabitants of various continents spread to attain their present distribution. But there is much, particularly in the biogeography of mountain and island communities, that cannot be interpreted in this fashion, at least in the present state of our knowledge. As far as creationism is concerned, knowledge and theory in this area have scarcely progressed in over a century.

b. *The Fossil Record.* Fossil stratification, although not as regular as the evolutionists would have it, has nevertheless been a lot more regular than creationists have thus far adequately been able to account for. We really ought to see more in the way of "anachronisms" in the fossil record than we do find if the stratigraphic segregation of fossil communities is indeed basically ecological. What *was* the ecology of the pre-Flood world? What distribution did organisms then have? To what areas was the human race confined, if any? Exactly what forces produced the fossiliferous strata we find today? Can we develop a coherent geological theory that will predict and explain better and in a greater variety of instances than current ones do? Creationism will have reached a new level of maturity and will command new respect when creationist geologists leave their armchairs to do such things as guide a drilling rig to a deposit of oil that conventional geology says should not exist.

c. *Human "Evolution."* Granted that the various fossil hominids may not be ancestral to modern man in the majority of cases, how do we explain their occurrence and characteristics? Where do the limits of animal behavior lie? How can we reliably differentiate between highly sophisticated animal behavior, particularly that of which the fossil hominids may have been capable, and human behavior? It is noteworthy that the most cogent criticisms of sociobiology, and the clearest perception of its threat, have come not from Christians but from Marxists.

d. *The Origin of Species.* If evolution can account for the formation of at least some species, can it not account for the formation of all of them? Are some species still in essentially the same form as when they were created? If so, which ones? Is differentiation above the level of species possible by evolutionary mechanisms? If so, what are its limits? If not, can we prove it? If it is possible, has it actually taken place or is it merely an academic possibility?

e. *Comparative Anatomy and Embryology.* Can we explain the occurrence of vestigial organs *better* than the evolutionists can? There is an immense catalog of them to investigate. Why do wisdom teeth exist? Human ear muscles? The dewclaws of dogs? Can we explain the phenomena of analogy and homology better than the evolutionists can? Can we show the necessity of a myriad of embryonic organs that have no obvious function in the adult but that are similar, often in detail, to those in the adult state of allegedly ancestral organisms? Why, for example, must the human embryo possess, in succession, *three* kinds of kidneys?

f. *Convergence of Evidence.* As much as anything else, evolution convinces by brute force. The total weight of evolutionary arguments is staggering. The *evidence*, though, is another matter, because it can be interpreted piecemeal in nonevolutionary ways. Yet the time comes when the mind tires of that approach and views it as unconvincing. Logically, ten unsound arguments demonstrate truth no better than one, but there is good reason for our instinctive feelings to the contrary. We usually find it unlikely that a multitude of convergent arguments will all be wrong. Could it be, many wonder, that the evolutionists are explaining the evidence while the creationists are explaining it away? "Cosmic ray bombardment *may have* been different in the past; the earth's magnetic field is *purported to be* decreasing rapidly with time; a vapor canopy *may have* covered the earth before the Noachian flood; the content of nitrogen atoms in the atmosphere from which radiocarbon is obtained by cosmic ray bombardment *may have* been different in the past; the radiocarbon clocks *may have* been going faster in the past," and on and on. Thus creationists are satirized by an evolutionist in a recent article.* We need to be less hypothetical. What is needed is to identify the cause or causes that have worked together to produce the kinds of systematic errors we suspect the evolutionists suffer from (there certainly have been other such instances in the history of science). We need not only to criticize the arguments for evolution but also to produce a credible explanation of why this evidence is as mutually consistent as it appears to be.

5. *Creationism needs determination.* In our day creationism has at last come out of the closet, and it is doubtless better for the airing it has received. Yet we must not confuse the unaccustomed success that some have achieved in debate for real intellectual victory. We speak of the creation "model," but should not a model show a close correspondence to the reality it is supposed to represent? The construction of a detailed model, comparable in scope to the theory of evolution that we hope to replace, has hardly begun. Yet we cannot expect to compete effectively with evolution unless we construct such a model. The overwhelming detail with which evolution is replete contrasts discouragingly with the almost complete lack of positive discourse in creationism. We must not allow ourselves to be either overconfident, as we have sometimes been, or discouraged, as we soon might be as the opposition warms more fully to the rebuttal of our claims.

Indeed we can take an example of determination from the evolutionists themselves. Despite their insistence that evolution is a falsifiable proposal, they have been unwilling to accept its falsification by any objection, however cogent, or counterexample, however damning, that has ever been proposed. Instead, evolutionists have with the most indomitable determination steadfastly refused even to consider abandoning their position. They have unfailingly and systematically developed counterarguments to the most telling blows that have been aimed at evolutionary theory. Their behavior stems from a heartfelt, almost moral commitment to the validity of their worldview. Can creationists afford to have a lesser commitment to the truth of God's Word?

This list is by no means exhaustive or necessarily the most appropriate one. It does include some things that have vexed us for

---

*Irving M. Klotz, "Why Not Teach Creationism in the Schools?" *Bioscience*, May 1982, p. 334.

years and which, if we had the necessary funds, time, and ability, we would like to explore ourselves. But 1 Corinthians 12 states that God has placed specialized members in the Body of Christ as He has pleased. Somewhere in the church there are probably men and women with the abilities needed. If you believe you may be one of them, 1 Peter 4:10 may provide the spark you need to get busy.

APPENDIX

In recent years there has been renewed interest in creation, and very pertinent and accurate literature has been produced both by secular and religious writers. Listed below are some of the leading publishing organizations and/or publications that are creation-oriented and worthy of the attention of those concerned about the subject:

Acts and Facts
Institute for Creation Research
P.O. Box 2666
El Cajon, CA 92021-9982

Bible-Science Newsletter
Bible-Science Association (national organization with many
    branch chapters)
2911 East Forty-second Street
Minneapolis, MN 55406

Biblical Creation
Biblical Creation Society
51 Sloan Crescent
Bishopbriggs, Glasgow
Scotland G64 2HN

Creation
Creation Science Movement (formerly Evolution Protest
    Movement)
"Rivendell," 20 Foxley Lane
High Salvation, Worthing
West Sussex BN13 3AB
England

Creation-Health Foundation/Creation Medical Fellowship
19 Gallery Centre
Taylors, SC 29687

Creation Research Society Quarterly
Creation Research Society
Membership Secretary
2717 Cranbrook Road
Ann Arbor, MI 48105

Creation-Science Research Center
P.O. Box 23195
San Diego, CA 92123

Creation Social Science and Humanities Quarterly
Creation Social Science and Humanities Society
1429 North Holyoke
Wichita, KS 67208

Faith and Thought
The Victoria Institute
29 Queen Street
London, EC4R 1BH
England

News and Views
Missouri Association for Creation, Inc.
P.O. Box 23984
St. Louis, MO 63119

Origins
Geoscience Research Institute
Loma Linda University
Loma Linda, CA 92354

Students for Origins Research
P.O. Box 203
Santa Barbara, CA 93116-0203

FOR FURTHER STUDY

Chapter 1

Darwin's life is summarized in a pleasant, interesting, and on the whole accurate fashion in a historical novel, *The Origin*, by Irving Stone (New York: Doubleday, 1980). *Darwin and the Beagle*, by Alan Moorehead (New York: Harper and Row, 1969) is an abundantly illustrated retelling of Darwin's voyage that helps to recapture the flavor of the times and circumstances. An excellent biography of Wallace is contained in *A Delicate Arrangement*, by Arnold Brockman (New York: Quadrangle/Times Books, 1980), which also makes the controversial suggestion that Darwin stole the idea of natural selection from Wallace, falsifying his memoirs to conceal the intellectual theft. One might also read Darwin's *The Origin of Species and Descent of Man* and *Voyage of the Beagle* themselves, which are available in many editions. A critical introduction to *The Origin of Species* (by W. R. Thompson, a Roman Catholic biologist) appeared in a 1956 edition. That introduction, still worth reading, has been republished by the British Creation Science Movement (formerly the Evolution Protest Movement).

Evolution as it is understood today is summarized in a variety of textbooks written for college courses on the subject. One is *The Science of Evolution*, by William D. Stanfield (New York: Macmillan, 1977). The specific philosophical and theological influence of Darwinism is explored in *Darwin and the Modern World View*, by John C. Greene (New York: New American Library, 1963), and more critically by the creationist authors R. T. Clark and J. D. Bales in their book *Why Scientists Accept Evolution* (Grand Rapids: Baker, 1966).

Creationism itself is the subject of many books, most of them by creationists, although some critical attacks on creationism are now being mounted by evolutionists. One typical example of an attempted evolutionist rebuttal is "The Creationists," a special section by several authors that appeared in *Science* 81, (December 1981, pp. 53-60). Unfortunately, it is very difficult for creationists to gain an opportunity for reply to such attacks that appear with some regularity in the popular science media. However, anyone seriously seeking credentials as a creationist should familiarize himself or herself with the typical approach of such criticism. Among anticreationist books we may list *The Monkey Business*, by Niles Eldredge (New York: Washington Square, 1982); *Darwinism Defended*, by Michael Ruse (Reading, Mass.: Addison-Wesley, 1982); and *Abusing Science: The Case Against Creationism*, by Philip Kitcher (Cambridge, Mass.: MIT, 1982). A sample of general creationist works might include *The New Creationism*, by Harold Clark (Review and Herald, 1980), *Why Not Creation?* by Walter Lammerts (Grand Rapids: Baker, 1970), and *Darwin, Evolution and Creation*, edited by W. Rusch (St. Louis: Concordia, 3d ed. in preparation). This last one is our special recommendation. The history of creationism is summarized with surprising fairness in "Creationism in 20th-Century America" (*Science*, 218:538, November 1982).

Chapter 2

There is a plethora of books on the fossil record written by evolutionary paleontologists, but exceedingly few by creationists. One of the best is *Fossils in Focus*, by J. Kerby Anderson and Harold G. Coffin (Grand Rapids: Zondervan, 1977). The question of the identity of the original Genesis "kinds" has been discussed by one of us in "What Are the Scientific Possibilities for Original Kinds?" by Wayne Frair, *Journal of the American Scientific Affiliation* (March 1958, pp. 26-30). An aspect of the fossil record considered by evolutionists one of the best weapons in their arsenal is what they consider to be the fossil record of the modern horse. "A Note on the Unsatisfactory Nature of the Horse Series of Fossils as Evidence for Evolution," by Frank W. Cousins, *Creation Research Society Quarterly* (8:99-108, September 1981) attacks and explodes the evolutionary interpretation of the horse fossil record.

Chapter 3

For an incisive criticism of the orthodox evolutionary interpretation of biochemical and other evidence, one can hardly find a better source than *Implications of Evolution*, by G. A. Kerkut (New York: Pergamon, 1960), although an updated version is badly needed. The author, though himself an evolutionist, points out many weak spots in the general theory of evolution. This book is a must for all biologists. A more recent science book treating data not reconcilable with Neo-Darwinism is *The Nature and Origin of the Biological World* (New York: John Wiley, 1982). Authored by E. J. Ambrose, an English scientist, the book also treats the matter of chance (and a Creator).

We have said little in this book about chromosomal studies as evidences for evolution. The reader who is looking for a fresh challenge could look at the comparative method as applied to chromosomes. Designed as an explicit attack on creationism, *Chromosomes, Giant Molecules and Evolution*, by Bruce Wallace (New York: Norton, 1966) should convey some idea of the challenge yet to be faced by creationism in this area, and it could stimulate someone to make a major contribution to creation science in rebuttal.

Though it is rather dry reading, the best summary of modern taxonomic models that we know of is "Biological Classification: Toward a Synthesis of Opposing Methodologies," by Ernst Mayr, *Science* (214:510-16, October 1981).

Chapter 4

A quick introduction to the saltationist theories of evolution can be found in "Miracle Mutations," by John Gliedman, *Science Digest* (February 1982, pp. 90-96). Steven Stanley's *The New Evolutionary Timetable* (New York: Basic Books, 1981) is a more thorough apology for one of these views, punctuated equilibrium. For a creationist critique see "Punctuated Equilibrium and the Macromicro Mutation Controversy," by James A. Melnick, *Creation Research Society Quarterly* (18:22-25, June 1981).

We have already remarked that we are not geologists and are not qualified to evaluate the validity of Flood geology and other geological proposals by creationists. Bearing that in mind, we suggest that Dr. Henry Morris is probably the leading modern advocate of Flood geology. Along with Gary Parker he has written *What Is Creation Science?* (San Diego: Creation-Life Publishers, 1982), which contains a recent summary of his views. Dr. Morris has also published a number of other books on the subject. Continental drift is discussed by G. Robert Morton in "Creationism and Continental Drift," *Creation Research Society Quarterly* (18:42-45, June 1981).

Another major article, which also considers the argument from distribution of organisms, appeared in two parts in the *Creation Research Society Quarterly* in 1979 and 1980, respectively. This is

"Biogeography from a Creationist Perspective," by George F. Howe and Walter E. Lammerts (in 16:38-43 and 17:4-18).

Chapter 5

Lifecloud: The Origin of Life in the Universe, by the noted British astronomer Fred Hoyle and N. C. Wickramasinghe contains much of interest to creationists, but is not really a creationist book. The authors believe life originated not on the early earth but in intergalactic space. The book is worth reading for it does contain cogent and incisive criticisms of the orthodox spontaneous generation views of the origin of life. A more recent book by these authors is *Evolution from Space* (New York: Simon & Schuster, 1981). The more "orthodox" evolutionary view is presented by Francis Crick in *Life Itself, Its Origin and Nature* (New York: Simon and Schuster, 1981), though Crick is a panspermist.

For an explicitly creationist view, see "Chemical Evolution," by Rene Evard and David Schrodetzki, *Origins* (3:10-37, 1976), "Organization and the Origin of Life," by John C. Walton (4:16-35, 1977), and "Hemoglobin Structure and the Biogenesis of Proteins, Part II: Significance of Protein Structure to the Biogenesis of Life," by Gordon C. Mills, *Journal of the American Scientific Affiliation* (27:79-82, June 1975).

The endosymbiotic theory is discussed and advocated in *Symbiosis in Cell Evolution,* edited by Lynn Margulis (San Francisco: Freeman, 1981). However, writing in the journal *Bioscience,* David L. Nanney of the University of Illinois in Urbana called this book "a prosecutor's brief that uses tricks of special pleading to support a highly personal form of the hypothesis." For a critical view, see "Cellular Origins and the Three 'Primary Kingdoms': A Critique," by Kevin Anderson, *Creation Research Society Quarterly* (16:197-202, March 1980).

Chapter 6

There is little recent creationist literature on genetic theories of microevolution. It might be worthwhile to look at Rusch's book, which was mentioned at the end of Chapter 1. There is also some information on classical genetics and mutations in *Heredity: A Study in Science and the Bible,* by William J. Tinkle (Grand Rapids: Zondervan, 1970). An article by William J. Ouweneel, "Genetics and Creation Studies," *Creation Research Society Quarterly* (14:26-34, June 1977) will repay study. *Population Genetics,* by James F. Crow (San Francisco: Freeman, 1982) is rather heavy going for the general reader but certainly presents a complete summary from an evolutionary standpoint. Any college-level evolution text should contain a more easily understandable account (we might suggest *Evolution*, by Theodosius Dobzhansky, Francisco J. Ayala, and G. Ledyard Stebbins [San Francisco: Freeman, 1977]).

Chapter 7

How better to learn about sociobiology than from Edward W. Wilson himself? *Sociobiology, the New Synthesis* (Cambridge N.H.: Belknap Press, 1975) is a definitive summary of and apology for the hypothesis. (Wilson's bibliographies are also helpful to the student who seriously wishes to make sociobiology a research interest.) To form an impression of sociobiology's implications for Christianity see "Edward O. Wilson, Father of a New Science," by Jeffrey Saver, *Science Digest* (May 1982, pp. 84-87). It is also worth looking at certain chapters in *Ethology, the Mechanisms and Evolution of Behavior*, by James L. Gould (New York: Norton, 1982).

Ray Bohlin is one of the few evangelicals who have publicly responded to the threat of sociobiology. His article "Sociobiology: Cloned from the Gene Cult" appeared in *Christianity Today*, 23 January 1981, pp. 16-19. The journal *Faith and Thought* contains the article "Sociobiology," by Gordon R. Clarke (1979, 106:50-60). However, sociobiology is not all that menaces Christianity in the behavioral sciences. See also Ellen Myer's article "The Skinner Trap: Abolishing Man's Worth" that appeared in the *CSSH Quarterly* (4:8-20, Winter 1981).

Chapter 8

Two books that present and advocate human evolution are *Lucy, the Beginnings of Mankind*, by Donald Johanson and Maitland Edey (New York: Simon and Schuster, 1981), and *Missing Links, the Hunt for Earliest Man*, by John Reader (Boston: Little, Brown, 1981), both of which, incidentally, contain a clear discussion of radiometric dating techniques. The nearest creationist equivalent we know of is *Evolution or Creation*, by Arthur C. Custance (Grand Rapids: Zondervan, 1976). An article on the subject has appeared in the *Creation Research Society Quarterly:* "The Creationist and Neo-Darwinian Views Concerning the Origin of the Order Primates Compared and Contrasted: A Preliminary Analysis," by Dennis W. Cheek (18:93-110, September 1981). Since African paleoanthropology is developing very rapidly, one can expect all scientific writing on the subject to become swiftly outdated. More restricted in scope, the article "Unthinking *Homo habilis*," by Chris C. Hummer, *Creation Research Society Quar-*

terly (15:212-14, March 1979), may serve as a model for other studies of specific aspects of the fossil evidence taken as supporting evolution.

Chapter 9

A monument of orthodox biblical scholarship, *Exposition of Genesis*, by H. C. Leupold (Columbus, Ohio: Wartburg, 1942) is thorough, logical, and exemplary. A number of philosophically and theologically oriented books also have been published on the doctrine of creation. Perhaps foremost among these is *Genesis in Space and Time*, by Francis Schaeffer (Downer's Grove: Inter-Varsity, 1972), but we also recommend *The Creation Explanation, A Scientific Alternative to Evolution*, by R. E. Kofahl and K. L. Seagraves (Wheaton: Shaw, 1975), and *The Unity in Creation*, by R. Maatman (Sioux Center, Iowa: Dordt College, 1978). A more recent refutation of the higher critical theories of the alleged multiple accounts of creation in Genesis is to be found in "The Unity of the Creation Account," by William H. Shea, *Origins* (5:10-38, 1978). This study is especially apt in view of recent attacks on creationism that attempt to show that the Bible itself contains at least two contradictory accounts of creation.

Finally, though the need for creationist biological research is acute, some progress has been made in the field of education. We are happy to point to the production of a number of high school biology textbooks of excellent quality that have been written in recent years from the creationist viewpoint. If in 1925 John T. Scopes had been using *Biology, A Search for Order in Complexity* (Milford, Mich.: Mott Media, in preparation) he would have had considerably more difficulty in persuading the court that he had actually taught evolution to his classes, and we would have been spared the great monkey trial.

Index

Moody Press, a ministry of the Moody Bible Institute, is designed for education, evangelization, and edification. If we may assist you in knowing more about Christ and the Christian life, please write us without obligation: Moody Press, c/o MLM, Chicago, Illinois 60610